Reflective Readers

THE POWER OF READER'S NOTEBOOKS

by S. Travis Crowder

For Laura Robb

"Every book, every volume . . . has a soul.
The soul of the person who wrote it
and of those who read it and
lived and dreamed with it . . ."

—from *The Shadow of the Wind*
by Carlos Ruiz Zafón

Table of Contents

WITCH BOY
BLOOD WATER PAINT
HIDDEN
FROST

CHAPTER 1

Embracing Readers' Growth and Change

I sat across from several of my seventh-grade students who wanted to share their thinking about the reflection process. Notebook and pen in hand, I asked: How has reflection in class this year helped you as a reader and thinker?

> Reflection is the catalyst that sparks all students toward a truer understanding of the reading process, of interpretation, and of themselves...
> ***S. Travis Crowder***

Nathaniel explained, "When you asked us to reflect, it really made me start paying attention to what I was reading. It pushed me to read different genres."

"Yeah," Carlos said, "it was a different way to think about what we were reading. You know, it wasn't the same sorts of questions we've been asked before. It made you think about your book."

"I think that's why I liked it as the year went on," Kaylee said. "It helped us connect to real life and there wasn't a right or wrong answer."

As they spoke, I wrote quickly, trying to capture their responses, because they so beautifully illuminate the power of reflective thinking and the reason I wrote this book. I developed this book because I'd come to see that reflection is the catalyst that sparks all students toward a truer understanding of the reading process, of interpretation, and of themselves as readers.

What Reflection Is

Reflection is the story of learning. Like hand-drawn maps, with routes curving and bending with noticeable individuality, reflection gives contour to our experiences, and forms the geography of our thinking. If we listen closely to our own thoughts, giving ourselves space and time to think, we begin to sense where we might want or need to go next. Reflection shapes the landscape of any learning journey.

> Reflection provides students with clarity, direction, and an awareness of their reading selves.

In the Reader's Workshop, reflection provides students with clarity, direction, and an awareness of their reading selves, understanding that "books help us understand ourselves and the world around us, giving us glimmers of who we are and who we might become" (Barnhouse & Vinton, 2012, p. 6). Over time, students come to see:

- A clear narrative of their progress
- Stronger connections between all of their learning
- That their reading selves may be different from their social selves, or who they are in a family structure, and that their relationship with books has the potential to drive their lives in positive ways.

How Reflection Develops Across The School Year

These three outcomes are reached over the course of an entire school year, and become part of a student's life as a reader forever. Because this is such a gradual process, I organized this book's chapters to follow the chronology of the school year and of students' growing reflection skills. I cover the what/when/how details in this chapter and the next, and then arrange chapters into phases of the Gradual Release of Responsibility model. So, in chapter 3, we learn about the **I Do** of teacher modeling and getting started with writing in notebooks. In Chapter 4, the **I Do** is focused on learning about the readers in your room. In chapter 5, discover many **We Do** activities—shared experiences designed to have students tiptoe into the shallow end of response and toward the deep end of reflection. In chapter 6, it's time for student independence, the **You Do** of reflection, when readers are more intentional about reflection.

A Reader's Notebook is fertile ground, a place where students can develop a long-lasting relationship with books.

> With this book, I am taking you through a year of learning beside students as they navigate reflective thinking. I show the incremental journey that builds children's confidence, understanding, and joy.
>
> —S. Travis Crowder

Portrait Gallery of Student Growth

The heartbeat of this book is **The Portrait Gallery** in each chapter. Here, I showcase examples of student writing. Usually one is an earlier-in-the-year example, and another mid or late year, to show how readers progress in a year.

These excerpts are brief, so as not to overwhelm you with reading. They are also meant to assure you that it's okay if you see somewhat superficial reflection at first, as students need time to know their own minds and risk-take on the page. You will discover that each year, the class is different. One year, students went from 0-60, surprising themselves and me with their ability to reflect before the first frost hit. Other years, progress is slower, and more subtle. Yet even in the quieter years, the practice of reflection leads to important growth.

Special Note About Nonfiction

As you will see in the student samples of reflection, most relate to their fiction reading. I purposely didn't load the book with nonfiction examples because whenever I tried to add more, it seemed I was trying to make the book all things to all genres. I know in my heart that any teacher reading this work will be able to apply it to teaching nonfiction without my formal introduction. And perhaps more to the point, I believe that I am strongest and truest when sharing ideas for fiction with you and my students. That's my bias. All literature is worth its weight in gold, yet I think short stories and novels have a special place in middle school classroom in which I teach. Children from a much earlier age than we think are beginning to feel the ground shift in their lives, and quest to know who they are and what and who they can steady themselves with; fiction writers create out of these very same needs. The writer Sandra Cisneros in her memoir *A House of My Own* puts it this way: "We find ourselves at home, or homing, in books that allow us to become more of ourselves. Home is 'not just the place where you were born,' as writer Pico Iyer once noted, 'It's the place where you become yourself.'"

"We find ourselves at home, or homing, in books that allow us to become more of ourselves. Home is 'not just the place where you were born,' as writer Pico Iyer once noted, 'It's the place where you become yourself.'"
—Sandra Cisneros

 |

Knowing the Difference Between Response and Reflection

Reflection is a dynamic process. When we reflect, we look back at an experience and recall the details, of course, yet we also tune into how the experience has changed us. If I reflect, say, on a time when a friend helped me through a tough semester in college, with jokes and favorite snacks and late night conversations, I'm thinking about the friend, how young and vulnerable I was, how words of wisdom helped me move forward, how much I've changed, and maybe some things that friend taught me about life. Reflecting about reading is or ought to be a similar mix—we notice how we've changed and grown as the result of the book, what we've learned, and how it might prompt us to effect change, both in ourselves and the world.

This notion of reading and reflecting to influence is a far cry from reading to answer, to recall, to get a grade and move on. And so as you read these chapters, I encourage you to keep this high contrast in mind; reading-to-perform is like wandering in a rocky mountain range without a map.

> . . . thinking about a text begins as response but eventually grows into reflection.

In ways, reflection seems similar to a reader's response, and honestly, there is overlap. Responses tend to be students' initial reactions, when they focus on their feelings and connections to a text. In my point of view, thinking about a text begins as response but eventually grows into reflection. Take a look at the following entries, and think about what's different between Hunter's response and his reflection.

A Reading Response

I really enjoyed *Fahrenheit 451* by Ray Bradbury. I enjoyed how Montag changed from a book burner to book savior. Mildred was frustrating because she never really did anything, but I liked how Montag decided to do what he knew was right to do. He was the character I connected with the most. If I were in his shoes, I would have tried to do the same thing, but in a world where you are punished for having books, I don't really know what I would have done.

In the response section above, Hunter focuses on his connection to Guy Montag, the main character of Ray Bradbury's *Fahrenheit 451*. Notice that Hunter explains how he connects and even provides some supporting evidence, but a text-to-self connection lingers in response thinking.

A Reading Reflection

I read *Fahrenheit 451* quickly, but I realized I was going back and reading parts of it again. It wasn't confusing, it just slowed me down, but I didn't mind. It really made me think about how a society can create chaos in the lives of people by reprimanding them if they have something considered "illegal." What could be illegal about books? I love reading and couldn't imagine being in a world without them. It seems, though, that books cause people to think on their own and Beatty hated when people thought on their own. So I guess that was the point.

In the reflection section above, Hunter moves beyond response to mine his experiences and think about the experience of reading itself. Hunter expanded the response to include elements of reflection, including questioning the text, and considering how he relates to the book and determining the book's significance. He is using his response as a springboard to move into reflective territory.

Take a look at the list of questions below. What do you notice about one type of question versus another? To me, the questions that elicit responses tend to orient around a specific text, whereas questions meant to stir reflection tend to orient around the reader—her process, her life, the dynamic combustion between the author's ideas and her own.

Questions that Elicit Responses

How did this make you feel?

What surprised you?

What is your reaction to ________?

If you were this character, what would you do?

What are your opinions about a character's decisions?

Do you agree with this writer? Why or why not?

What big ideas do you notice in this piece of writing?

What evidence supports your thinking?

What argument does this author raise about _____?

How do you feel about this? Why?

Questions that Elicit Reflection

What did you notice about this piece of writing?

What trends have you noticed in your reading life?

Based on your reading life, what big ideas do you seem drawn to?

What questions do you have now that you've read this?

Why does this piece of writing/book matter?

Now that you've read this, what do you feel you need to do?

How do you feel you've grown as a reader because of this reading experience?

Will this help you affect change in your world? How?

Book-Head-Heart Framework

Kylene Beers and Robert Probst (2018) introduced the Book-Head-Heart framework in *Disrupting Thinking.* BHH is another way for students to think about the texts they read, especially as we teach them to be responsive and responsible readers.

BHH Reading
When you read, think about what is....

IN THE BOOK
What's this about?
Who is telling the story?
What does the author want me to know?

IN YOUR HEAD
What surprised me?
What does the author think I already know?
What changed, challenged, or confirmed my thinking?
What did I notice?

IN YOUR HEART
What did I learn about me?
How will this help me to be better?

Supporting Growth

This book clarifies the distinction between response and reflection for one important reason: when we teachers know the difference, we can take readers farther in the course of a school year. It's that simple. In the graphic shown here, notice that response and reflection are not on a continuum. Instead, readers ebb and flow between the two domains. In everyday life, even the most engaged, habitual readers may respond and move on from a text, for a host of reasons. For example, so-called beach and airplane reads may entertain us but not warrant reflection. Or we may be in a period of life when reading is meant to relax or even distract us from hardship.

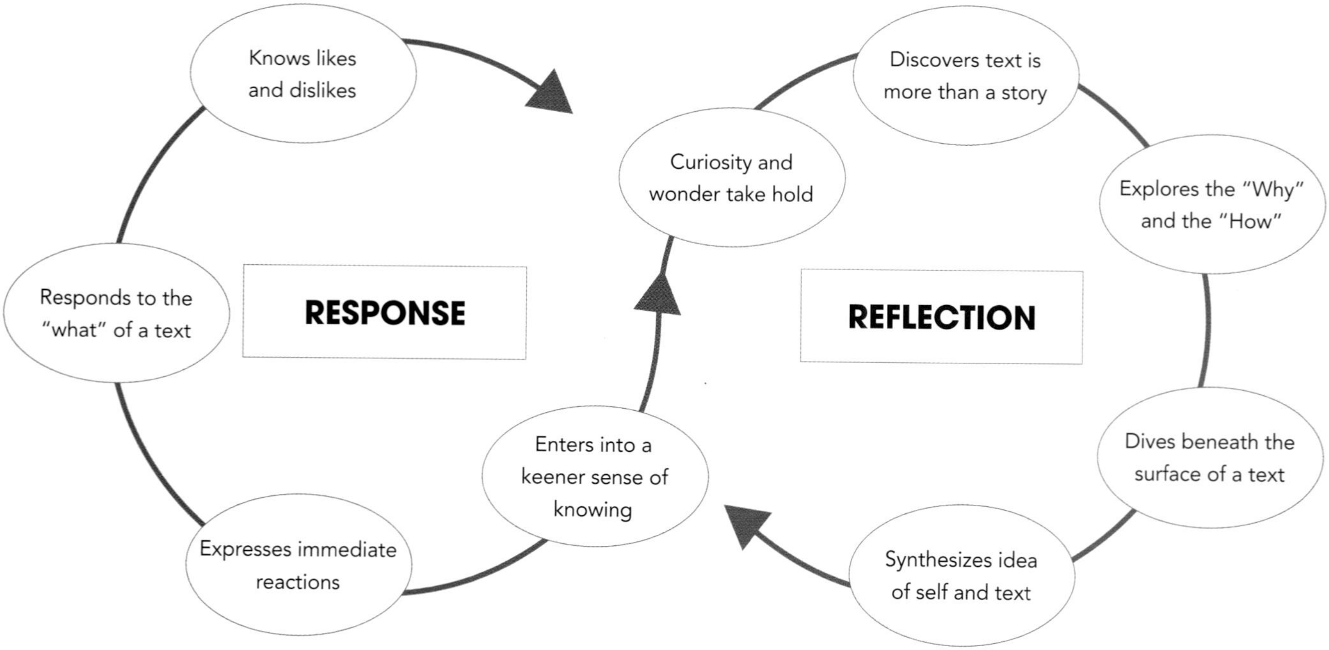

Core Beliefs in Action

As is true with all good teaching, all we do in terms of routines and practices are tethered to our beliefs about what it means to learn, and what we think our role is for our students. These beliefs develop from literacy research and experience teaching; never one without the other. The nine statements that follow represent the conclusions I have drawn from teaching, professional reading, and research on comprehension, social emotional growth, conferring, and reading motivation, among others. The day-to-day conversations I have with students and colleagues are what makes these beliefs matter, and solid as sun-baked earth. I encourage you to develop your own list of beliefs, in your own words. As you proceed through the book, you will notice these beliefs evident in the classroom practices.

TRY THIS

Develop your own list of beliefs about teaching and learning, in your own words.

Students admire their teachers when they know their teachers, and the beliefs they stand for.

We Learn Through Stories

My philosophy of teaching reading rests on the belief that all students love stories and want to deeply engage with them. In Robert Coles' words, it helps them to develop a sense of "sorely needed understanding" of their world and of the people who inhabit it (*The Call of Stories*, p. xiv). We carry our stories with us, and we bring those stories to the threshold of each text we encounter. And we need them. They help us interpret, providing a lens through which we understand the role of *character* in life, and that we are engaged in a hero's journey.

TRY THIS

Read aloud one moving picture book or short story per day for a week. As you do so, I want you to simply notice students' facial expressions as you glance up from the book or show them the illustrations.

Reading Develops Empathy

Reading engages the heart and mind. When a child connects to a book it shifts her into an affective plane where she can be moved by characters and interested in their struggles. She walks and she thinks beside the characters (or, with nonfiction, the people and the events), and as the characters grow and change, her comprehension and connection grow, too.

TRY THIS

Comb your classroom shelves for a book that you feel will elicit a strong emotional response from students. You may want to read aloud the picture book *Drawn Together* by Minh Lee and Dan Santat or a section from *A Long Walk to Water* by Linda Sue Park. Talk openly about your reactions to these books. Create an anchor chart that includes words of emotion and invite students to write or to talk with a partner about their own reactions. Discuss transfer— how can you move this into your own reading life and notice and name the emotions you experience when you read?

Reflection Flourishes with Trust

The development of students' reading lives, which is the primary goal of a Reader's Workshop, starts from a place of love and sustains with a respect for each student, so that mutual trust ensues. Why? Because inviting students to engage with texts and develop the habit of reading takes curiosity, compassion, and patience. As poet Eve Merriam said it so well, "it takes a lot of slow to grow." Some students will adapt quickly to a Reader's Workshop environment, while others will need time to grow into a reading habit and identity. And that is acceptable. Trust your teaching, trust your students, trust the process.

Develop a culture of reading, stoke peer work, and show yourself as a reader too.

TRY THIS

After a week of Reader's Workshop, invite students to write in their notebooks or turn and talk with a partner. Ask: ***What helped you during the week to fall into the story or language of your book? How do your interests intersect with the events, people, and/or ideas in the book? What do you notice about themselves as readers?*** **Encouraging them to express (with help from a peer and/or a class-created anchor chart) what they notice will give them a foundation for a year of reading.**

> "It takes a lot of slow to grow," Eve Merriam says. Trust your teaching, trust your students, trust the process.

Reading and Reflection Grow from Choice

Choice is a crucial element that changes students' perceptions about learning. When children can continually choose what to read, a schoolwide culture of reading is possible (Robb & Robb, 2020). Conversely, when schools rely on curriculum maps and sacrosanct reading lists that are assessment-focused and teacher-centric, students disengage from the act of reading, and fall further and further behind in their abilities as critical readers. In my classroom, reading and reflection grow from the choices students make. As students continue to make choices in their reading lives, we consistently consult the to-read lists inside their notebooks (discussed more in Chapter 2) to determine where they need to go next. To help students develop their own reading independence, I want them— no, I need them— to begin making choices on their own, using the resources, such as the reading recommendations in the fronts of books or a friend's suggestion, to guide their choices as readers.

TRY THIS

Consult your librarian, the Voya magazine or School Library Journal websites, or a trusted colleague for book recommendations for your students. Keep a list, either on your classroom door or on a wall in your room, that will showcase favorites.

Assisting students with book selection skills is central to their developing a vibrant reading life.

Reading Engages the Heart of the Mind

Books have the capacity to affect our hearts and minds simultaneously. When we invite students to read, we are inviting them into a process of heart and mind engagement. This conviction comes from my reading *The Heart of the Mind* by Michael Clay Thompson (2001), which woke me up to the false dichotomy that often dominates academic practices and curriculum development. Generally speaking, traditional instructional routines split the heart from the mind, and don't do enough to connect with students' interests. When we focus on relevant ideas and issues, share compelling fiction and nonfiction, and make it okay for students to think and feel as they read and write about their reading, we all excel.

TRY THIS

Do a one-minute Quickwrite about your teaching or your students in response to this excerpt from Regie Routman's *Literacy Essentials* (2018):

" . . . we must do whatever we can to first capture students' and teachers' hearts before worrying about how much we are instructing them. Have you noticed that no one ever says 'mind and heart'? That's because if we win a person's heart, the engagement, effort, and intellect are more likely to follow. To reach the heart, we appeal to people's interests, needs, and curiosity; respect their culture and background; value them as individuals; and care about their well-being (p. 77)."

From every vantage point around the globe, we need to open our hearts and minds together. Literature helps us to do that.

Reflection Leads to Recreational Reading Habits

If you look at common language arts curriculum, or report cards for that matter, it seems we define a successful reader as one who completes complex books, or a series of classroom assignments of some kind, and in general "participates" in school. *Participate* is such a wan word, isn't it? If we are serious about creating lifelong reading habits, might we drum up some more energy? Dream up a classroom environment that is more indie bookstore than institution? When I walk into a bookstore full of books and readers, it releases endorphins and I feel at home. The space is full of people in the habit of reading.

TRY THIS

Recall the palpable engagement in the air in a good bookstore or a library, and the buzz of endeavor —that's what we want to set in motion. To do that, from early in the year, try asking students:

- **Where do they want to go?**
- **How many books do they want to read?**
- **What genres do they want to explore?**
- **What do they want to know more about?**

Management TIP

Sometimes I pose these questions in the midst of discussion, but more often than not I encourage them to write about them in their reading notebooks. The happy side effect is that the students' reflection primes them to begin to develop personal reading goals. I'll go into more detail on how I demonstrate the process of writing in my notebook in more detail in chapter 3, but the gist is, I do it often, so that students see it's a habit of mine. Students writing in notebooks is the backbone of this book.

Reflective Thinking Needs to be Modeled

Students are curious about their teachers, so it makes sense to give them insight into your reading life. My notebook goes under the document camera almost every day, so students see how my words and pictures are my own peculiar emojis of response. I might muse about a genre or book I want to read next, an author I just don't seem to "click" with, what I want to accomplish in a week or a year, topics of great interest, and so on.

> My notebook goes under the document camera almost every day, so students see how my words and pictures are my own peculiar emojis of response.

My modeling never ends with a command of, "Now you try this." Instead, it's an explicit yet gentle invitation, a glimpse of what it is like to be in the habit of reading, and the pleasurable contest of goal-setting for oneself. I hope one day many years from now I will walk into a bookstore and see a person browsing in the New Releases section, and think it looks a lot like a former student—only to discover that it is.

TRY THIS

What book are you currently reading? Either under the document camera, on a piece of chart paper, or on your board, write a response that leads into reflection. Write about your feelings, how you've connected to a book, and what you've noticed about yourself as you've read this book. Consult "Questions that Elicit Reflection" (page 13) for other prompts. Invite students to share what they notice about your writing. Make a list on chart paper and hang in your classroom for future reference.

Readers Need to See Reflection as Part of Reading

Once upon a time, I was a teacher who kept one eye on the clock and another on the curriculum map. I believed I was expected to cover material and in doing so, I wound up cantering through Shakespeare and Bradbury, ruining beautiful literature because I was obsessed with time and "getting it covered." The students who were victims of this horrid process did not develop a love of reading; in fact, they digressed and were never given an opportunity to flex their reflective thinking skills or find the texts that resonated with them.

Inviting students into a gathering space to discuss reading takes away the formality of teaching and learning. It demonstrates the power of community and how precious the social aspect of reading really is.

We cannot rush the reading process of our students. In *Proust and the Squid: The Story and Science of the Reading Brain* (2007) Maryanne Wolf notes how important pace is for readers: "In music, in poetry, and in life, the rest, the pause, the slow movements are essential..." (p. 213). She argues that the allegiance to "more" and "faster" should be met with vigorous questioning (p. 214) because that allegiance affects how we learn and how we think about our learning. All readers need time to process a text, and write about their thinking, and when given this opportunity, the quality of thinking grows. There is little more rewarding than watching students at the end of the year look back over the body of work they've created in their notebooks to appreciate how much they have changed as readers and thinkers. Rushing this process will only end in frustration, both for you and students. These slow moves, these pauses, are critical to students' fledgling reading lives.

We cannot rush the reading process of our students.

TRY THIS

Ask students to turn and talk about how their thinking about characters has changed since starting a novel. At first, student talk may be surface-level, so follow the turn and talk with time to write about their conversation or share with the larger group. Talking with peers is vital to reflective thinking development, so do these activities several times a week. This activity is easy to adapt for biographies and nonfiction.

Portrait Gallery of Student Growth

Brittani

Beginning-of-the-Year Reflection

Book: *Gym Candy* by Carl Deuker

This book (Gym Candy) is touching my heart because when Mick was angry about his dad lying to him it made me feel mad too. I want to read more books like this.

My Take: When asked to reflect about her first book of the school year, Brittani skimmed the surface. She reveals an impressive personal connection, and tiptoes into reflection territory with her last sentence, but like many students at the start of the year, she stops short of more expansive thinking about the novel and her experience of it.

TRY THIS

Digging into this reflection is essential— what separates this writing from being truly reflective? As students learn the ropes of reflective thinking, they will strive to reach into their hearts and minds to unearth deep thinking. When students admit that they want to "read more books like this," I want them to pinpoint the "what" of their statement. What did this book have that makes you want to go in search of others like it? A big idea? A problem? Helping students generate a list in their notebooks such as types of characters, problems I like to read about, emotions books help me experience, and so on guides them to do a better job of articulating the book elements they enjoy, and what they look for in future reading.

Middle-of-the-Year Reflection

Book: ***Dear Nobody*** **by Gillian McCain and Legs McNeil**

I am reading Dear Nobody. Mary Rose is an alcoholic and she is addicted to drugs. I feel bad for her because she had such a hard life and she didn't have many friends and she moved a lot. As I read this book, I am trying to put myself in her shoes. I need to read more books like this because I am interested in reading about how kids deal with these problems (drugs, etc.).

My Take: *In Brittani's mid-year reflection, her thinking has developed considerably. She lingers in response for a moment, but moves into reflection, thinking about how she had tried to put herself in the character's shoes and identifying the things she wanted to read more about. Although this reflection shows growth, I talked with her about stretching her thinking even more.*

TRY THIS

Nine times out of ten, the in-the-moment coaching I do takes the form of asking a question or two aimed at a line of thinking I am not yet seeing enough of. I might say, "What might you do now since you've read this book? What have you noticed about yourself since putting yourself in the character's shoes? How is this book changing you as a reader?"

Collegial Conversations

Reflective thinking creates permanence in students' learning (Keene & Zimmerman, 2007). In *Mosaic of Thought*, Ellin Keene and Susan Zimmerman (2007) convey the value of reflection sessions, a time when students gather and readers share what they have learned. Looking back across their reading lives, kids are given space and time to describe what they learned, as well as what they learned about themselves, both as readers and human beings (p. 134).

As students continue to think about their reading lives, considering the things they have learned through their reading and the ways they have changed as a reader, they develop agency—they are directing their own reading lives. They are the monitors and they decide where they are and where they need to go.

Supporting Change

To help kids think about their reading, in the first weeks and possibly months of the school year, I always start by inviting response. I ask:

- "How did this make you feel?
- What in the text made you feel that way?"

This response is just a beginning. My ultimate goal is for the response work to lead to students' considering how something has made a difference. To push their thinking further, I may ask them: "What do you feel is the meaning behind this text? In other words, why does this text matter? How have your reactions helped you understand the significance of this text?"

Considering questions such as these is, to me, true reflection—when we notice the inner changes and also notice whether the book has made us see the world differently. This work moves us into the "so what?" territory of reading and thinking, when our thoughts turn to "what should happen" once we are finished with the reading.

Sometimes this after-reading exploration takes the form of rereading the text. At other times, we might look back across our experience as a reader, perhaps even skimming earlier notebook entries, to appreciate that how we experienced this current book is far different than how we responded to that book, earlier in the evolution of our thoughts and skills as reflective readers. This "after" work might involve others and it might inspire us to act—to write to the author, write an editorial, dabble in that genre as writers, dive deep into that genre, and so on. All because we've noticed the inner changes. Only when we notice the inner change can we act wisely in the world.

TRY THIS

To invite readers to stretch their thinking, read their notebook responses, and then ask questions in conferences like, What did this novel tell you about yourself and what do you feel you need to do and/or read as a result of this reading experience? (See chapter 6 for more details.)

Inner Change and Outer Change

I think the concept of inner change and outer change is key; we don't talk enough in the reading profession about the fact that avid readers are those who embrace the tumultuous, ever-changing state that reading puts us in. Reading is meant to knock us off our feet, to change us, to alter how our minds work about an issue or theme. Reflection is the process that helps us regain our footing through thinking and writing down our flying ideas and reflecting to a point that they become insights. These insights are both evidence of growth and change and proof of a steady, sure reading self.

Just as we teach students that long passages in a novel, when we get the protagonist's inner thoughts, often signal major character conflict and growth, the sentences in our notebooks are the hallmarks of change for us too. A friend told me that when she was in college, the poet Richard Wilbur visited the campus and read aloud his poem "The Writer" and she was so moved by it that she went back to her freshmen dorm room and cried, wrote about it one of her beat-up spiral notebooks. She found the notebook decades later and was astounded by how powerfully the reflection itself brought back the emotional impact of the poem, and helped her see all the changes in her from then to now, as a reader and a person. Literature prompts inner and outer change—and reflection does too.

A Reflection

"Out of My Mind by Sharon Draper made me feel different about people who are handicapped. I used to think they had to have everything done for them. It looks like I was wrong. People with disabilities can do anything! I really want to read more books like this."

—Vivian, Fifth Grader

QUESTIONS *to* ASK YOURSELF

- **Can you think of a time in your own life when reflection was really important? Why?**
- **How does reflection challenge all of us to go deeper in our thinking and maybe even problem solve? How can it help you and your students?**
- **How can your insights about reflection in your own life help you model and coach reflection with your students?**

Further Reading

Here are a few of my favorite professional books on reading response:

Teaching Reading in Middle School
by Laura Robb

Reading with Presence
by Marilyn Pryle

The Write to Read
by Lesley Roessing

Response and Analysis
by Bob Probst

Notice and Note
by Kylene Beers and Bob Probst

Concluding Thoughts: Belonging

In this chapter, the following points have been explored:

- Response and reflection are separate processes, but they do overlap, and so we must honor student response in order to nudge them toward reflective thinking.
- Engaged readers think back across their experiences and use those experiences to guide them—in the now and in the future.
- Stories unite us all, and when students adopt a reading life, they are becoming part of conversations that reflection will help them understand more intimately.
- Reflection nurtures students as readers and thinkers.

I believe that we need to embrace the way that reading can disquiet us for a spell, before we reflect and in a sense tame the rawness of our response. Readers make sense of what the author stirs in us. We frame it so we can better learn from it, and act upon it. So, in conclusion, let reading spur us to act. Let reading and reflection change us as readers and humans.

It's only fitting then that I share the work of Kaylee, who told me that the reflections she wrote in her notebook and voiced during conversations with me caused her to reread *The Outsiders* by S.E. Hinton. The rereading experience got Kaylee thinking about mistakes. In a subsequent reading conference with me, she noted that so many characters in the book ponder their mistakes. It got her thinking about her own mistakes, which had created some personal turmoil for her this year. She also penned a poem that I continue to use as a Quick Write text with students.

MISTAKES

We all make mistakes
We all get punished from them
We learn from them
Hopefully not do them again
I think it depends
On the mistake you made
Big?
Little?
Bad?
Very Bad?

We all make mistakes
After the damage is done
You get a title
It could be a popular kid
Bad Kid
Cool Kid
Your parents see you differently
Other family members
Teachers
Classmates

We all make mistakes
But most days I wonder
Wonder why
Why I did something so stupid

Kaylee, Seventh Grader

THE WITCH BOY

CHAPTER 2

Connecting Reflection to Workshop Routines

Now we turn from the Why of reflection to the grounding details of exactly when you bring reflection to your readers. You bring it in via the four main strands of literacy— reading, writing, speaking, and listening— which you engage in each day. Students are given time to read, write, study, craft, and share (Kittle & Gallagher, 2018), although the minutes devoted to each strand are adjusted daily depending on the needs you see. That is, you plan each class period using observation and conference data, so there is some variation in the schedule, but for the most part it's predictable. I have used this schedule for the last three years and have found it incredibly beneficial in structuring my classes and keeping students organized.

> **Reader's Workshop** is a setting and a mindset. In this chapter, I share a weekly workshop schedule that works beautifully, and show you how to link teaching to your readers, their reflections, and their current curiosities and needs.
>
> *S. Travis Crowder*

Sample Weekly Schedule

Monday	Tuesday	Wednesday	Thursday	Friday
Book talk (3-5 minutes)	**Book talk**	**Book talk**	**Mini-lesson** How do we use changes in character to understand the theme of a story?	**Book talk** (student-led)
Mini-lesson e.g., on noticing changes in character (10-12 minutes)	**Independent reading**	**Independent reading**	**Independent reading & check-ins** (look for connections to the big ideas we unearthed yesterday)	**Independent reading & check-ins** (How has your thinking changed since yesterday? Do you see anything different?)
Independent reading & check-ins (15-20 minutes)	**Mini-lesson:** What do changes in character tell us? How might these changes be connected to big ideas?	**Time for response:** What do you need to write about?	**Time for response:** What do you need to write about?	
	Independent reading & check-ins	**Poem study:** "Mother to Son" by Langston Hughes (Noticing qualities and traits in characters)	**Notebook response:** Choose one of the big ideas we unearthed and connect it to your book. Find two examples that will support your choice.	**Discussion:** How do changes in character show us big ideas?
Notebook responses: What changes have you noticed in your character? (5-10 minutes)	**Time for response in notebook:** What do you need to write about?	**Create anchor chart:** What big ideas live inside the poem? (hardship, struggle, perseverance, determination, etc.)		**Reflection:** Writing about Reading
Share w/partner (5 minutes)	**Talk w/partner:** What might the author be telling us with this character's changes?	**Whole-class discussion:** What big idea do you feel is represented the most? How did it change the speaker or possibly make the speaker see things differently?	**Discussion:** How are these examples related to characters' changes?	Collect notebooks every two weeks to gauge students' understanding of skills, content, and ability to reflect.
Debrief & takeaways (last minutes of class)	**Debrief & takeaways**	**Debrief & takeaways**	**Debrief & takeaways**	

The Components of Reader's Workshop

Reflective thinking permeates our familiar routines. Notice in how I describe my use of the components of workshop that they hug the Gradual Release of Responsibility Model of instruction (Pearson & Gallagher, 1983). In the graphic shown below, developed by Adria Klein (2017), she adapts the model to emphasize the goal of learners transferring new understandings, independently, in new situations.

As you read on in this book, the lesson ideas and strategies will also mirror this teaching and learning model. Teaching reading, reflection, writing— virtually anything— is a process of an expert (teacher) showing a more novice learner (student) how to do something new. The expert slowly "releases" the task to the learner as he sees the learner's capacity for doing the task grows.

I develop my students' reflective thinking through teacher modeling (I Do), shared practice with support (We Do), and then having students reflect on their own (You Do). This is never an entirely linear process; it ebbs and flows. For example, your student might do something independently and continue to need support, especially as the student reaches for ever more sophisticated iterations of what you've taught.

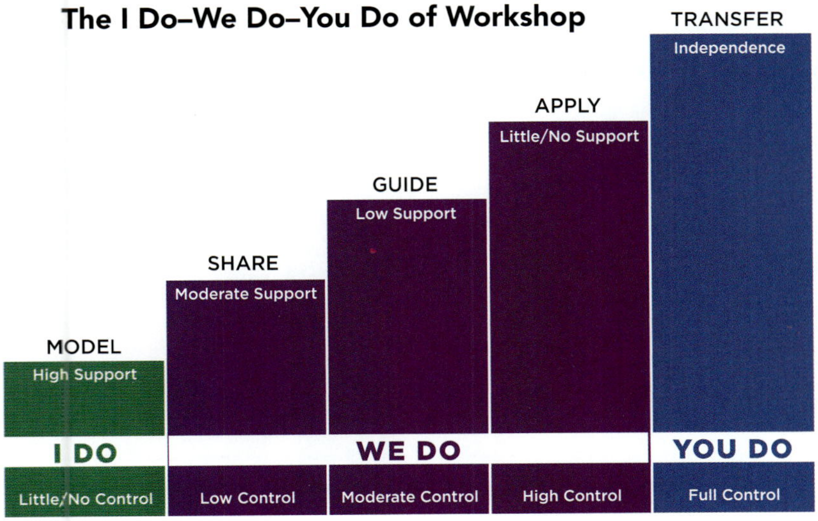

Book Talk (3-5 minutes)

Book talks are brief yet engaging talks about books and, in the words of Teri Lesesne (2010), their purpose is to sell students on the idea of reading them (p. 43). Kids read the books we bless, and through our conversations with them, they hear our enthusiasm. I choose books based on students' interests. Standing before my class, I hold the book so they can see the cover clearly, give them a brief summary that leads up to the problem in the story, and select a section to read aloud to them. In time, I hand over some of the book-talking responsibility to the students.

Book talks by teachers and students keep a steady flow of compelling fiction and nonfiction in everyone's sights.

How Book Talks Help

As a teacher, I rarely shy away from controversial topics. I keep age-appropriateness in mind, of course, and "read the room" in terms of my students' life experiences, but I believe children intuitively know that diversity strengthens the world. As educators, we have a responsibility to bring the wider world to our students. Here is a list of some novels that deepen our thinking on humanity:

Fourth Grade and Up

- *Wishtree* by Katherine Applegate
- *Blended* by Sharon M. Draper
- *Insignificant Events in the Life of a Cactus* by Dusti Bowling
- *Front Desk* by Kelly Yang
- *Esperanza Rising* by Pam Muñoz Ryan
- *El Deafo* by Cece Bell
- *Crenshaw* by Katherine Applegate
- *Long Way Down* by Jason Reynolds
- *Ghost* and the other books in the series (Jason Reynolds)
- *The Bridge Home* by Padma Venkatraman

Fourth/Fifth Grade and Up

- *Refugee* by Alan Gratz
- *Unbound* by Ann E. Burg
- *Out of My Mind* by Sharon M. Draper
- *Ghost Boys* by Jewell Parker Rhodes
- *Wonder* by R.J. Palacio
- *A Long Walk to Water* by Linda Sue Park

Middle School and Up

- *The Whispers* by Greg Howard
- *Dear Martin* by Nic Stone
- *The Hate U Give* by Angie Thomas
- *The Marrow Thieves* by Cherie Dimaline
- *Speak* by Laurie Halse Anderson
- *Shout* by Laurie Halse Anderson
- *Just Mercy* by Bryan Stevenson
- *Amal Unbound* by Aisha Saeed
- *Internment* by Samira Ahmed
- *Tradition* by Brendan Kiely

Think back to when you were a young reader. How did you find your way to a favorite book?

Connection to Reflection

One of the most rewarding challenges for a teacher is helping students develop a reading identity. Many come into my classroom without an understanding of their reading selves— their genre preferences, allegiance to authors, and topics that will fulfill them. Book talks give kids an opportunity to consider their interests and think about whether the book intersects with those interests. At the same time, book talks nudge children to stretch themselves as readers when the book appeals, even though it seems outside their "natural habitat" as readers.

Possible Teaching Points

1. Choose a piece, perhaps a section or an entire chapter of a book, that you know will resonate with kids. I have often made the mistake of just reading the first chapter, but this arbitrary choice does not often move kids to add the book to their reading lists. Select a piece from the book that will give them a reason to read it. You may also choose to supplement your book talk with a book trailer. Many can be found on publishers' websites, as well as YouTube.

2. Think aloud how this book has affected you, modeling for students how our responses are important and naming how you feel about a text.

3. Keep a running list of books you book-talk across the year and post it in your room. Students need reminders of these books, and a list will help them remember the books you've discussed and the memories and emotions associated with those books.

Management TIP

Each class period involves some form of reflection, but there is a caveat: Too much reflection is exhausting, and once the reflective process is overused, students are not very forgiving. Reflection should be used to extend and deepen thinking, not as an on-demand daily activity after each portion of Workshop.

Independent Reading (15-20 minutes)

During this time, students read a self-selected book tied to their interests and curiosities. I use this time to meet with students—asking about their reading and focusing on their contributions to the conversation. I find out how the reading itself is going, what helps them in terms of habits or strategies, how the book makes them feel, their wonderings, and the things they love or dislike about the story and/or the characters. This also gives me a chance to check in (see next page) to assess students' comprehension of texts and to help them further their reading skills, such as making inferences, unpacking unfamiliar vocabulary, making predictions, and analyzing characters.

> Independent reading time ought to feel more like free, student-owned time for choice reading than a school period.

Connection to Reflection

Engaged, independent reading itself involves reflection. Reading helps one reconnect with oneself, for it's a time when the mind of the author, the hearts of the characters, and the reader's own voice, mind, and heart come together.

Possible Teaching Points

1. Independent reading time ought to feel more like free, student-owned time for choice reading than a school period. So the teaching that you do is mostly through check-ins with readers.
2. Use what you glean from check-ins to note future, needed mini-lessons.

Using Check-Ins to Assess Comprehension

Brandon entered my classroom with an established disdain for reading. I knew because he told me on the first day of class how much he hated reading. It took me a short while to realize that Brandon's resistance to reading was born from his difficulty with comprehension. Yet with my support, he started reading graphic novels, then began reading what I call hybrid novels, such as *The Last Kids on Earth* series and *Diary of a Wimpy Kid*. I sat beside him a lot in those first weeks of school, asking him to tell me what he was reading about. "Hey Brandon," I would say, "would you mind talking to me about the book you're reading?" He would smile and start chatting about the book. To make sure he was grasping the story, I asked him to point to places in the text that helped him arrive at conclusions about characters and the plot. This quick check-in provided me with the evidence I needed to assess and scaffold his reading comprehension.

3. Trust the choices that students make as readers, but don't forget to encourage them to challenge themselves as readers. During check-ins, take them back to the notes from the mini-lessons and ask if there are strategies or ideas that will help them dig deeper into the text, such as looking at characterization, big ideas, argument, making inferences, or unpacking vocabulary. Let them know that they have a treasure chest of strategies to help them read.

Check-Ins

A check-in, commonly referred to as a reading conference, is a time I speak with students about their reading. As students read independently in the classroom, I will take 3-5 minutes to meet one-on -one. Honestly, though, to ensure I am reaching every student, I also check in with students as we are walking to the cafeteria, getting ready to change classes, or as students are coming to class in the morning. I will ask them how their reading is going, what's happening, and what they are thinking about as they read. It's critical as teachers that we break free of this idea that conferring only occurs during independent reading.

We teachers are always listening to our readers with a few things in mind. Although assessing and teaching comprehension isn't the focus on this book, it's often a focus of check-ins.

 |

Connection to Reflection

I use this check-in time to actively listen— to really hear what students are thinking, what's going on in their minds as they read, and what background knowledge they are connecting the book to. These check-ins help students think through their responses, determine where they are in their reading journeys, and feel mentored by me.

Possible Teaching Points

1. Empower students with language to define their responses and reflections. Help them notice and name what's happening. For example, if you see students are starting to connect big ideas across several texts, help them name that. "You're starting to notice big ideas in your book," I'll say. Then we'll talk about the big idea and the evidence that supports it.

2. Send students to write in their notebooks when something significant occurs during a check-in. For example, if a student begins to uncover a big idea, I will tell the student to go to her Reading Response section (see page 61 for details on each section of notebook) and write about the big idea she noticed. Additionally, if a student begins to determine *why* a certain book matters, I encourage him to go inside his notebook and write down his thinking. I might prompt with questions like "Why do you feel this book matters?" and "Now that you've uncovered that, what should you do?"

> These check-ins help students think through their responses, determine where they are in their reading journeys, and feel mentored by me.

Reading and talking about books doesn't always involve deep reflection in my classroom. Writing reflections is not an every-day, every-book event.

3. Keep check-ins as brief as possible so you can get to all your students. Ask students if you can join their space and let them do most of the talking. Open-ended questions such as "What are you thinking about?" keep students thinking and talking about their books and releases the responsibility to them— they own their reading experiences and need to be the ones deciding what they say. Such a question also helps keep the conversation brief because it is a student-centric question— not overladen with academic language that students might find threatening and not aimed at finding a "right" answer.

Mini-Lesson (8-10 minutes)

The mini-lesson is many things, but it's always brief. Keep it under 10 minutes, or run the risk of zapping its effectiveness. Teachers model comprehension strategies, reading habits, and a big armful of other literacy skills. In the context of helping students to deepen their reflective thinking, I use my own experiences with books as fodder for my mini-lessons. I encourage you to do the same, because just as teachers need to write in front of students, teachers need to read and reflect in front of students.

The mini-lesson is many things, but it's always brief. Keep it under 10 minutes, or run the risk of zapping its effectiveness.

The goal is to move students from passive to active in a workshop environment. Again, keep in mind that not all students will use the ideas from a mini-lesson immediately; instead, think of them as an addition to their strategy toolkit. Nancie Atwell (*Naming the World*, 2006), after sharing a poem with her students, offers a "benediction"— closing comments that leave them with ideas of how they can infuse elements from the text they just studied into their own writing.

Think of mini-lessons as a time to do that—offer ideas for ways students can make their reading stronger.

A Reflection

"I read *The Crossover*. I liked it because I play basketball too. I was sad at the end because his dad died. I wish he would not have died."

–Deb, Fifth Grader

Connection to Reflection

During mini-lessons, students are introduced to or revisit a skill. In Reader's Workshop, mini-lessons equip students with ways to interpret and analyze texts, such as understanding character, making inferences, using context clues to define an unfamiliar word, and so on. I encourage students to think about skills that they have mastered or ones they are striving to understand more deeply.

Possible Teaching Points

1. Use mini-lessons to help students develop an understanding and awareness of reflective thinking. Create an anchor chart listing the differences between response and reflection (possibly using the Questions that Elicit Responses and Questions That Elicit Reflection on page 13) to help students better grasp the nuances of both.

2. Use check-ins (i.e., conferences) with students to determine the skills you need to address during the mini-lesson time. For example, if students are striving to understand how character and theme are related, use the mini-lesson time to help them understand the relationship.

3. Give students time to reflect on the mini-lessons. Pose questions such as: How will this lesson help me interpret texts? What do I need to help me be more successful?

Management TIP

Keep mini-lessons short but specific. If you give explicit instruction for longer than 15 minutes, it is no longer a mini-lesson; it is a lecture. Mini-lessons about theme, argument, figurative language, and vocabulary are important, but always go with what readers need and with what you think will help your current group of students be successful. For more on reading mini-lessons, see *What Do I Teach Readers Tomorrow?* by Gravity Goldberg and Renee Houser.

Notebook Responses

After reading, students need time to capture their thinking. I do not ask students to write a response every day, but I do ask them to write often, usually three times a week. I use the Questions that Elicit Responses box (page 13) to guide my choices for reading responses. As students' abilities to respond to their reading mature, I ask them to "listen" to what their hearts and/or books might be urging them to write about, such as a character, a question, a wondering, or a problem. For students who need more guidance, I provide a question/prompt for them to consider as they respond to their books.

Writing about reading requires a place, sufficient time, and a classroom culture that honors the relative quiet that creative thinking needs to flourish.

 |

Connection to Reflection

Writing responses in notebooks (or anywhere!) leads toward reflection. By inviting students to notice and name their responses to books, identifying how books make them feel, they can then also reflect on *how* and *why* they feel that way.

> Tell students to let their pencils find the thinking.

Possible Teaching Points

1. The esteemed journalist Donald M. Murray said, "You write to discover what you want to say." (1981). Let kids know that the more they write, the more ideas they find. Tell students to let their pencils find the thinking.
2. Share responses to your personal reading with your students. Place your notebook under the document camera and talk kids through your process of responding to your reading. Even better— write extemporaneously about a book you are reading and let them see you find ideas and write as they watch.
3. Hold on to exemplary responses from students. Linda Rief (2014) suggests giving students packets of students' notebook responses from years past and asking them to comb through them— paying attention to the things they notice about the responses. Students need to see possibilities for responding and reflecting, and here, mentor texts work beautifully.

Management TIP

I do not ask students to write a response every day, but I do ask them to write often, usually three times a week.

Readers and writers each day need collaboration with peers.

Whole-Group Discussions

It's true— we come together to read texts often. It's usually a shorter piece, such as an article, poem, or excerpt from a larger work. After we read it, I often leave students with a thought and encourage them to go back inside the text to identify the things that surprise them, or appreciate descriptive language, or character descriptions, or— when working with nonfiction— lines that point to the author's argument. We come together to discuss what they notice.

Connection to Reflection

Whole-group discussions provide prime opportunities to engage students in talk about their noticings and how they read a text. Ask: What did you notice about yourself as you read this? What strategies helped you unpack this text? This is yet another place where students can carry skills from this experience to their own independent reading lives.

Possible Teaching Points

1. If using a whole-class or shared text to generate whole-group discussion, choose something that is intellectually stimulating, relevant, and demanding for your readers.

2. If you are using students' independent reading to stimulate conversation, have students respond in their notebooks first, then open the class up to discussion. Asking kids to respond to theme, author's craft, or argument in their reading will help them frame their ideas in writing *before* sharing with the whole class.

3. Before initiating a whole-group discussion, think about having students turn and talk about what they've written first. Some students need time to frame their ideas with a partner before sharing with a larger group. This also gives quieter students a chance to think and talk about texts.

 |

Questions to Float After a Read-Aloud

After a read-aloud, I like to create the feeling of an ellipsis . . . rather than a hard stop. Doing so helps readers make the transition into the next part of the day, and invites them to savor the story they just heard. I do this by leaving students with a thought, such as:

So much in this text has helped me understand myself— as a reader and as a thinker. I want you to consider the ways that this author has affected you. When you read, notice how an author moves you as a reader and thinker.

Alberto Manguel says: "Reading letters on a page is one of its [reading's] many guises. The astronomer reading a map of stars that no longer exist; the Japanese architect reading the land on which a house is to be built so as to guard it from evil forces; the card-player reading her partner's gestures before playing the winning card; the dancer reading the choreographer's notations; the weaver reading the intricate design of carpet being woven . . . all these share with book-readers the craft of deciphering and translating signs" . *This is a wonderful take on reading! I invite you to be aware of all the times you are reading; reading the stars, reading expressions, reading music, and reading someone's mood.*

Consider the descriptive language and how it helped us see the setting. How might you use description in your own writing? How might this author's craft help you?

Sandra Cisneros says: "Write what makes you different." Authors often write about the things that set them apart from others. I want you to consider your reading life. To what extent are you reading texts that make you different? As you continue to grow as a reader across this year, I want you to consider how your reading life sets you apart.

Debriefs and Takeaways

I love for students to have time to share their thinking in the last 5-to-10 minutes of class. This is a perfect time to help students name a strategy they've used or encourage them toward deeper reading. Asking questions, such as "What have you experienced as you've read and talked today?", encourages students to identify the intersections in class where their thinking has improved or they've made progress as a reader.

Connection to Reflection

Reflection is a recursive process— students look back at their reading, experiences, and accomplishments again and again to help them in the moment and gear up for future reading. These debriefs help them determine what in particular has helped them, how they've grown, and what might be a logical next step in their reading lives. Hearing peers' insights gives them inspiring ideas and language too.

Hearing peers' insights gives them inspiring ideas and language too.

Possible Teaching Points

1. Look to connect the debrief to the mini-lesson or whatever shared experience transpired. For example, if your mini-lesson was on noticing characterization or identifying argument in a text, discuss with students at the end of the mini-lesson how they can read to determine the strategies that will help them. For example, if they are reading a book that is character-driven, such as *The Book Thief* by Markus Zusak or *The Giver* by Lois Lowry, they will want to use strategies to help them unpack character to understand the book more deeply. The strategies might comprise looking at dialogue, passages of internal dialogue, and scenes of character upset and change. By contrast, plot-driven books, or those with complex, shifting use of time, might require strategies attuned to flashback, synthesizing, and re-reading at moments of confusion.

 |

2. Ask a student to share with the class a powerful moment you noticed as students wrote in their notebooks or something you heard or noticed during a check-in. Introduce this to the class by saying, "During a check-in, I listened to one of your classmates talk about an interesting theory he had about the novel (or nonfiction). I want him to share that with you and also tell you how he arrived at that theory." Students hear what another student noticed and can use that student's understanding to lift their own.

3. Use the debrief time to coach students. Encourage more timid students to share their ideas and coach them as they share their thinking. You might say, "I'm noticing that you're sharing a lot of how you're arriving at your ideas" or "Wow, Josselyn, you're sharing so much of your responses to this book! What do you think you need to do because you've read this work— keep reading more texts like it or write something?" These conversations at the end of class help students notice, name, and start owning the language of response and reflection.

Invite readers to share their reflections with the class.

Friday Reflections

Friday reflections provide time for kids to think about their week of reading. As students get better at reflecting, I turn the responsibility over to them and let them choose the tool—freewrites, hashtags, or Tweets— they use as well as when they reflect (see more about tools in chapter 5). I do, however, want to protect this Friday reflection time. After independent reading, I want students to consider their week of reading and think about what they've accomplished.

Exemplary Reflections

The Prompt: WHEN THINKING ABOUT YOUR READING LIFE . . . (Freewrite)	I have noticed that my reading life has grown this week because I have read 30 pages more than last week. I am finding time in the afternoons when I get home to read and as I read, I keep my notebook near me so I can jot down my thinking. I've also noticed that when I read with my notebook open, I am paying more attention to the language the author uses.
The Prompt: WHEN THINKING ABOUT YOUR EXPERIENCES AND NEXT STEPS AS A READER . . . (Tweet)	I have been filled with anger while reading Angie Thomas's T.H.U.G. this week. I'm beginning to understand why it's important to take action. #BLM is a critical mvmt, & Starr's story is helping me see that. I believe I need to read more about #BLM.

Connection to Reflection

This is the time for focused reflective thinking, when students can look back at their reading responses and the notes from the mini-lessons and think about what they've accomplished and what they think they need to do as readers. This is also a time for them to consider how their reading lives are changing. Take a look at the two powerful examples, shown at left.

Possible Teaching Points

1. Model a reflection in your own notebook under your document camera or on a piece of chart paper for students to see.

2. Be transparent about your own reading reflection— thinking aloud answers to such questions as: How has your reading life changed and how have you grown? What do you notice when your reading life stagnates?

3. Demonstrate what you want from students in the form of reflection through think-alouds and feedback inside of their notebooks. When you read student notebooks, underline noteworthy thinking, encourage them toward deeper thinking with a simple "tell me more" comment, and keep an anchor chart of exemplary reflections in your room. You may even consider photocopying excellent reflections from students and sharing them.

Management TIP

During check-ins with students and independent work time, be on the lookout for things students might want to share with peers. Have a space in the classroom, such as a special chair, a rug, or other space, where students can stand or sit to share their work. I often ask students to slide their notebooks under the document camera so their peers can see the work they've created. Allow this time to be as student-centric as possible.

Portrait Gallery of Student Growth

Naveah

Middle-of-the-Year Reflection

Book: *Because I am Furniture* by Thalia Chaltas

#summarize #competition. This connects to my book because she is competing against other teams.
#roughlife. This connects to my book because she has a lot of family problems

My Take: *Naveah's hashtags are creative, but her thinking is limited in her mid-year reflection. She is making connections with a big idea, but I would love for her to dig into the family problems a bit— what is she noticing and how is this affecting how she sees the characters? She might make stronger connections between her hashtags as a place to start. I would ask, Do you think there is a connection between the character's competititveness with sports and her rough home life?*

TRY THIS

Many students skate across the surface of texts before doing analytical thinking, and so as a teacher you want to keep asking complex questions that compel complex thinking. For Naveah and any student, prompt them to more aggressively pursue connections between actions, responses to events, protagonist and supporting characters. "Does one thing influence another?" "How might what happened here relate to what happened there?" Do a lesson with a short text to model how to move from hashtags to analytical thinking.

End-of-the-Year Reflection

Book: *Campfire* by Shawn Sarles

Part 1- Freewrite and Hashtags

#fear #suspense #realism I am enjoying this book because it's very realistic and at the end of every chapter, it has a cliff hanger and makes you want to keep reading the book.

Part 2- What have you experienced?

I have experienced not knowing what would happen and I have experienced me being scared of not knowing what would happen.

My Take: *By the end of the year, Naveah was taking the time to consider her reactions, and what they revealed to her about herself as a reader. During a reading check-in, I talked with her about our emotions, an idea that came up in several mini-lessons, and how we can use those emotions and reactions to guide our reading lives. She was hesitant to trust her instincts, but this reflection shows that it does take a lot of slow to grow. She finally wrote about her experiences as a reader and discussed with me how that feeling of realism is something that she looks for in her reading life.*

TRY THIS

We want to move students farther into reflection that considers the Why and the How. Why do you feel this way? What author craft moves were behind it? What in your life fed this emotion? How does the author pull this off—character dialogue, evocative description? Exploring the combustible materials between self and text not only strengthens comprehension skills, it develops a reader's awareness of author and genre preferences. Naveah's recognizing her affinity for realistic fiction is huge. Going forward I will keep asking her to also reflect on how her thinking and writing has grown.

The mother of all Reader's Workshop components is— you guessed it— the book. Authors including Penny Kittle, Lester Laminack, Renee Houser, Laura Robb, Linda Rief, Kylene Beers, Donalyn Miller, and Jennifer LaGarde have given depth and breadth to our awareness of texts for independent reading, and I encourage you to read their work on this topic. Following are 10 tips culled from their wisdom to help you load your classroom library with books that reflect students' vast interests and identities:

1. Stock wordless picture books, picture books, poems, short story collections— the operative word here is short. Many readers love these briefer reads on their way to longer text.
2. Know your students' interests. Use interest inventories (see page 87) to guide your selection process.
3. Post a **Classroom Library Suggestions Chart** in your classroom for students to add book titles. Give them time to browse related and suggested titles online.

4. Know middle-grades and young-adult literature for yourself. Spend time reading and reflecting on the books that you know students will love and cherish. Kids read the books we bless, so be intentional with the books you read and share with your children.
5. Be familiar with different formats, such as graphic novels and novels in verse.
6. Include a focus on nonfiction, giving students a chance to see that nonfiction is not always dense. Show them intriguing narrative nonfiction such as *The Boys in the Boat* by Daniel James Brown, *Brown Girl Dreaming* by Jacqueline Woodson, *The 57* Bus by Dashka Slater, and *Born a Crime* by Trevor Noah. Let them see that there is a gorgeous heartbeat inside of informational texts.
7. Consult trusted websites, professionals, and resources for book titles that will enhance the quality of your classroom library, bringing fresh and diverse voices to it. We Need Diverse Books is an organization that identifies, endorses, and advertises books of diverse authorship. Use Harnessing the Power of Incombustible Ideas: Tips for Creating Inclusive School and Classroom Library Collections checklist (LaGarde & Crowder, 2018) to help assess the diversity of your selections. (Checklist found at: https://nerdybookclub.wordpress.com/2018/02/16/incombustible-ideas-the-subtle-bigotry-of-book-banning-by-jennifer-lagarde-and-travis-crowder/)
8. Take an inventory of your classroom library and identify the missing voices and perspectives. Be aware of your own bias when purchasing books.
9. Set up your classroom like an indie bookstore. Have "student picks" where kids write an endorsement for a book and tape it underneath. Books can be arranged— cover forward— on counters or on bookshelves around the room for other students to see.
10. Leave reviews— from Goodreads and students— inside the front covers of books. Encourage students to look there for a review that will entice them to walk away with the book, itching to dig into the story.

Digital Resources

The classroom library is a part of the instructional heartbeat. Use interest inventories, recent releases, award winners, and websites to build and curate a print and digital library.

We Need Diverse Books (https://diversebooks.org)

The Adventures of a Library Girl (www.librarygirl.net)

Nerdy Book Club (www.nerdybookclub.wordpress.com)

School Library Journal (www.slj.com)

VOYA (www.voyamagazine.com)

Riffle Books (www.rifflebooks.com)

BookTrib (www.booktrib.com)

The Brown Bookshelf (www.thebrownbookshelf.com)

American Indians in Children's Literature (https://americanindiansinchildrensliterature.blogspot.com)

Latinxs in Kid Lit (https://lantinosinkidlit.com)

Rich in Color (richincolor.com)

Colours of Us (coloursofus.com)

Concluding Thoughts: Beginning

In this chapter, the following points have been explored:

- Reader's Workshop is based on choice as well as routine—book talks, independent reading, mini-lessons, time for response & reflection, whole-class discussions, and feedback.
- Students need time to read and to write about their reading in order to develop the habits associated with reflective thinking. Book choice and access are critical first steps!
- Your role as the literacy leader in your classroom is to listen to what your students need by leaning into their notebook responses, their comments during whole-class discussions, and check-ins.

Students need time to read and to write about their reading in order to develop the habits associated with reflective thinking.

Being clear on how we spend each valuable minute is good; it's not that we don't want flexibility, but teachers and students alike thrive on predictability. The beauty of Reader's Workshop routines is that they authentically, easily address the four main strands of literacy: reading, writing, speaking, and listening.

Further Reading

Here are some of my favorite professional texts about Reader's Workshop:

Seeking Diversity and *Read Write Teach* by Linda Rief

Book Love by Penny Kittle

The Book Whisperer and *Reading in the Wild* by Donalyn Miller

Teaching Reading in Middle School and *Read Talk Write* by Laura Robb

Sparks in the Dark by Travis Crowder and Todd Nesloney

In the Middle and *Naming the World* by Nancie Atwell

The Reading Zone by Nancie Atwell and Anne Atwell Merkel

To Know and Nurture a Reader by Kari Yates and Christina Nosek

QUESTIONS to ASK YOURSELF

- **How do conversations about our reading help us make more meaning out of the books and texts we read? How might it help your students?**
- **Read for 10-15 minutes and, once you are finished, jot down your thinking in your notebook. Pay attention to your process: What did you write? What did you think about? How did writing extend your reading experience?**
- **How might your answers to the questions above influence your students? Is there value in sharing your own reading process with the kids in your classroom?**

NO EASY DAY
FERAL YOUTH
When We Collided
PAPER TOWNS
HOW IT WENT DOWN
BECAUSE YOU LOV
JOHN IRVING
ALL RISE
No Fear
Walk Two Moons
THE BOOK THIEF
GRENADE
FRANKIE
THE WIND IN THE WILLOWS
THE STARS BENEATH OUR FEET
VIOLENT ENDS

CHAPTER 3

Introducing Students to Notebooks

> Our first move is to help students understand that without a reader, a book has no utility.
>
> ***S. Travis Crowder***

Now, let's look at how the Reader's Notebooks are set up, and how to introduce them to students. The short story is, students almost always need to be introduced to the "why" behind notebooks, because they often haven't used them or haven't used them to their fullest potential. In fact, too many readers in our classrooms believe that texts operate independently of the reader. Quizzes, standardized tests, and traditional five-paragraph essays have led them to assume that a book has a prescribed meaning. By extension, a notebook that holds reflections—a Reader's Notebook—is mystifying to many kids at first. So our first move is to help students understand that without a reader, a book has no utility. And without a place to reflect, a reader may not find the emotional/intellectual space for deep connection to texts.

A Place for Thoughts to Land

Above all, let students know they matter. They matter as young individuals, and they matter as readers. In *Literature as Exploration*, Louise Rosenblatt (1995) wrote eloquently about the substance a reader brings to a text. She stated, "The instructor's function is . . . to help students realize that the most important thing is what literature means to them and does for them" (p. 64).

Students need a place to write their reactions and reflections about the things they read. In my classroom, the Reader's Notebook (Rief, 2007) is the place where students hold that thinking. To help you deepen your sense of using notebooks, I have organized the how-tos along the **I Do—We Do—You Do** of the gradual release of responsibility model. Generally, the first weeks of school are heavy on the **I-Do** of teacher modeling.

Kaylie's notebook cover announces a wonderful mix of what she holds dear about life.

What You Might Say

I introduce students to notebooks during the first week of school. I begin by talking about what it means to live a readerly life. I convey that readers are people whose lives are drenched with story, and they have drive and direction as consumers of narrative and information. Many readers, like me, keep a notebook with them when they read, and when a sentence, a character, an idea, or a moment captures their attention, they make that thinking visible inside their notebooks. If you teach students younger than seventh grade, you can, of course, modify the language I suggest here, but it amazes me what kids in elementary can "get" when we expect them to.

Books take us on flights of imagination, tours of our own hearts, and shake us out of our own points of view. And all that leads to wisdom.

I mention that I carry my notebook with me everywhere, because that's what I do as a reader and writer. I need students to recognize the gravity of such thinking. We are not reading arbitrarily—we are reading to respond and reflect.

Often, students come to my class believing that texts operate independently of the reader. They have been given the impression that a book possesses a prescribed meaning and does not need the reader, the one who interacts with it. Reader's notebooks help them realize how much they bring to the text, that they bring it into being.

> "The instructor's function is . . . to help students realize that the most important thing is what literature means to them and does for them."
> —Louise Rosenblatt

I DO Sharing Your Teacher Notebook

A notebook tour (Gallagher & Kittle, 2018) is a powerful introduction for students. I place my notebook under the document camera and talk about how I use each of the four sections.

The sections of the notebook provide readers with separate but interrelated spaces in which to reflect. They are adapted from *Inside the Reader's-Writer's Notebook* by Linda Rief (2007), who has deepened the world's thinking through many professional books, mentoring, and teaching.

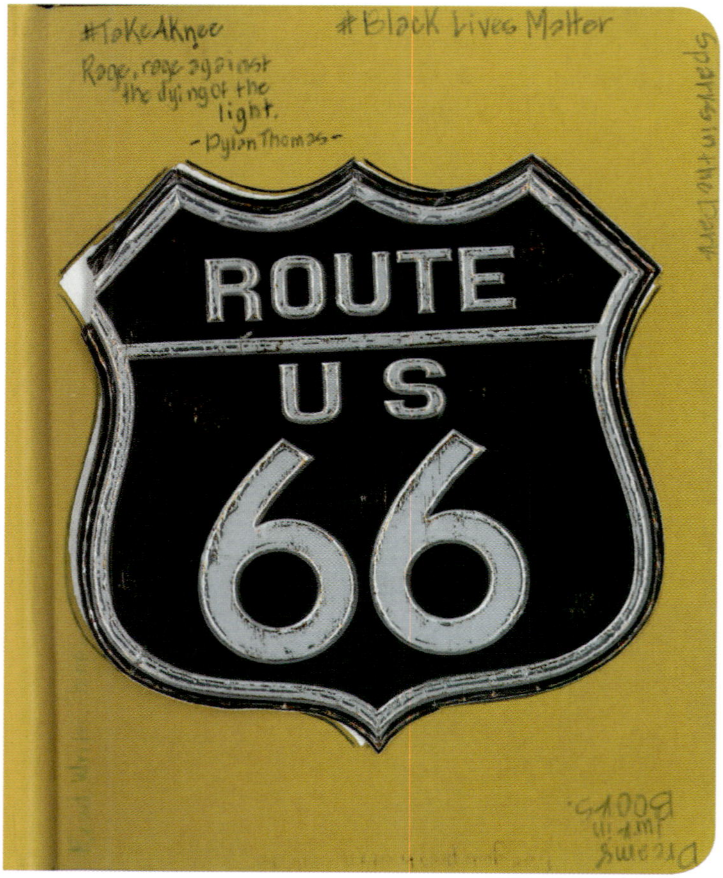

Stephen's cover reflects his wanderlust with books, that "there is so much to travel, so much to discover," and reading can take you there. Jack Kerouac's spirit lives on!

1. To-Read List

You might say: "In this section, add titles of books you would like to read, or may want to read. Get suggestions from book talks, friends, and browsing the classroom library."

How this section evolves over time: Take three-to five minutes at the beginning of each class to talk about a book that you feel your students would enjoy. The first several months of school are filled with multiple book talks, but as the year progresses, the book talks are turned over to students.

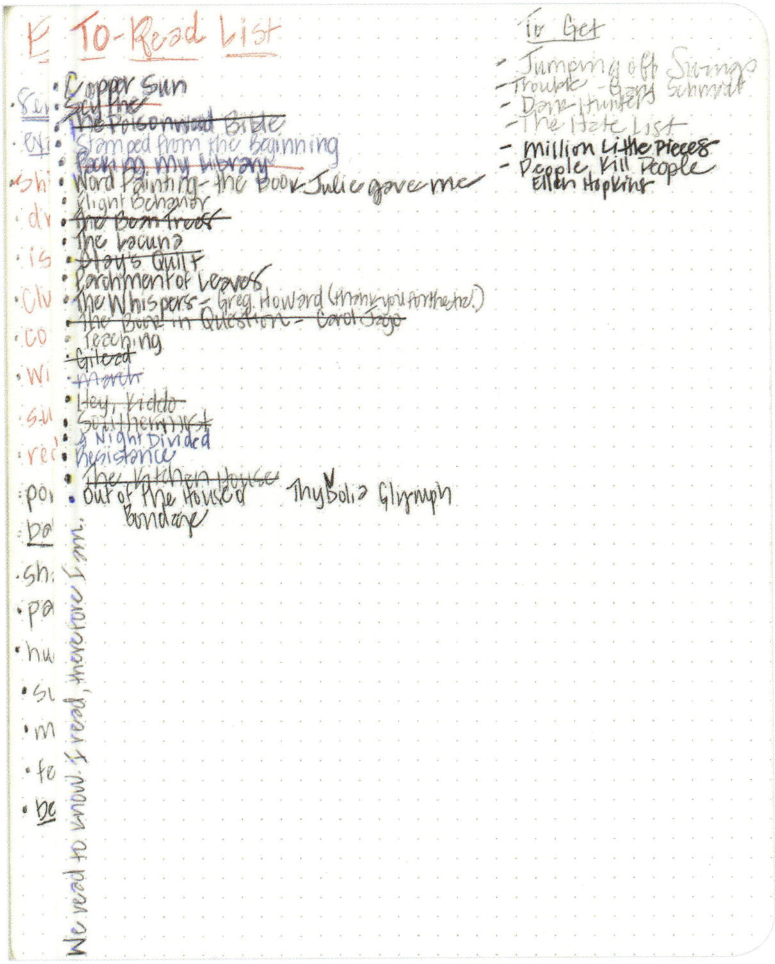

The "To Read" page of my notebook.

2. Reading Responses

You might say: "Here in this section, respond to what you are reading, both independent reading and shared texts. This space is also used for your weekly reading reflections each Friday."

How this section evolves over time: Students should be responding to texts daily, but I do not require that all responses be written in the notebook as such expectations may create resistance. Just 2–3 days each week for short bursts of thinking in the reading response section after independent reading is adequate.

I happen to like adding illustrations to my notebook, but whether my students do is entirely their choice.

 |

3. Writing

You might say: "Here is where you will write longer and more creative pieces related to your reading. In writer's workshop, you can use this same section to grow pieces of writing."

How this section evolves over time: As students begin building pieces based on their reading (two-page spreads, intertextual connections, pieces related to big ideas, and so on), this space within the notebook will be used often. Allow time for this space to be used as needed when students become comfortable with creating their own two-page spreads or other larger pieces of writing related to their reading lives.

This section houses writing about reading. For Writer's Workshop, students also use this section to write seeds of ideas that may grow into larger pieces.

4. Vocabulary

You might say: “This section is for words that strike you or that come up in class. Collect words from independent reading and our shared reading. Skim this section periodically and you might find words you want to use in your writing.”

How this section evolves over time: Make word study a regular part of the classroom (daily if possible), and allow time for kids to marinate in the language of their reading lives.

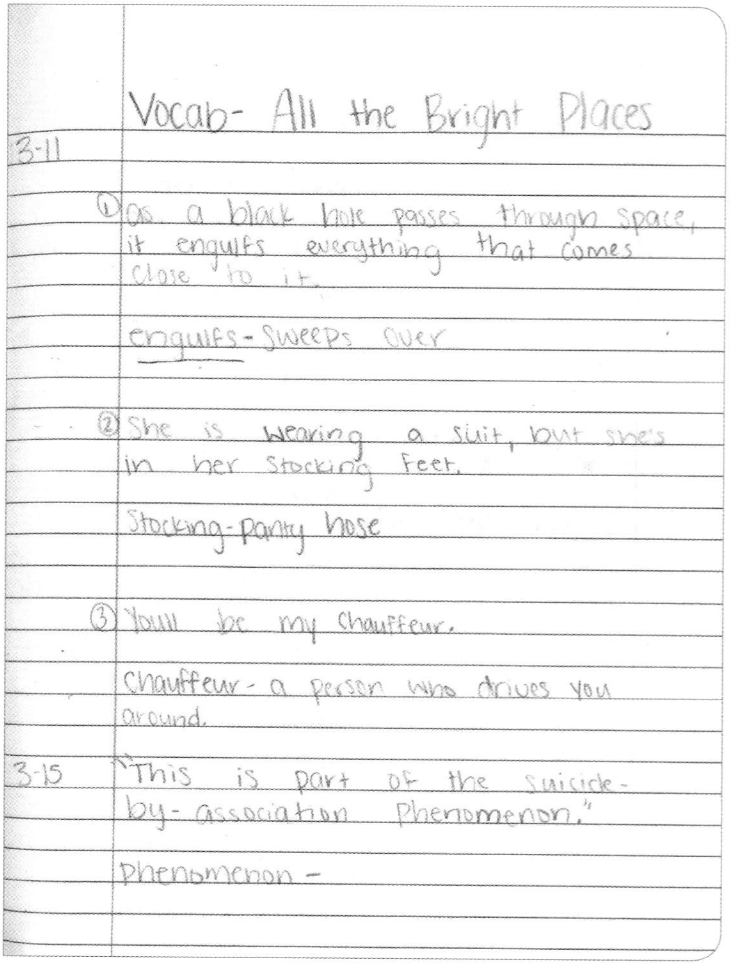

Authors are masters of language, so it makes sense to connect students to their well-spoken words.

Wrap Up

You might say: “I want you to consider how this notebook can be used this year to guide you as a reader, writer, and thinker. I’m going to give each of you a sticky note. Choose a section of your notebook you feel most drawn to now, such as one you’re curious about or one that stands out above all the rest. On the sticky note, briefly write how you think this section will help you grow as a reader. Put your name on the back of the sticky note. When you’re finished, place it on the inside cover of your notebook. I will look for them when I collect your notebooks.” When students have had time to write, let them turn and talk with a partner or share their ideas with the whole class. We learn from sharing our ideas.

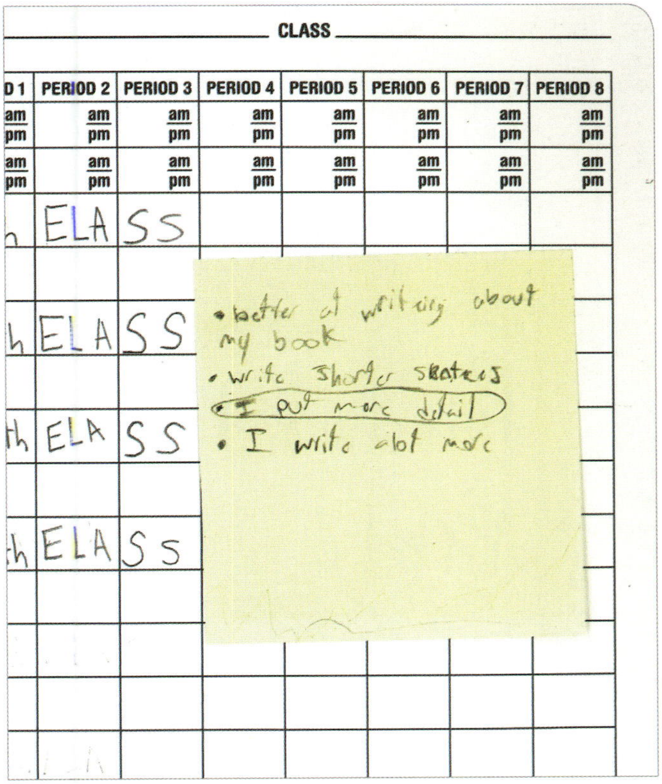

A student considers how a section about writing will help him think more deeply about the books he reads.

I DO Creating Two-Page Spreads

It is early September, a day or two after my notebook tour lesson. I am in my classroom with my notebook open to an entry I'd done a few weeks earlier on Barbara Kingsolver's *The Poisonwood Bible*. Based on an idea I adapted from Penny Kittle (2018), I often create two-page spreads of beautiful words I have taken from books because these sentences and phrases are filled with ideas that I want to collect and spend time with. My students are engaged in independent reading, so I pick up my pen, and write around the collected sentences and words, thinking about ideas, my choices as a reader, and what I notice about the various pieces of the novel I selected. I listen to the things that land on the page. As a result, a palette of reflective thinking comes into existence. On a whim, I decide to share my process with students.

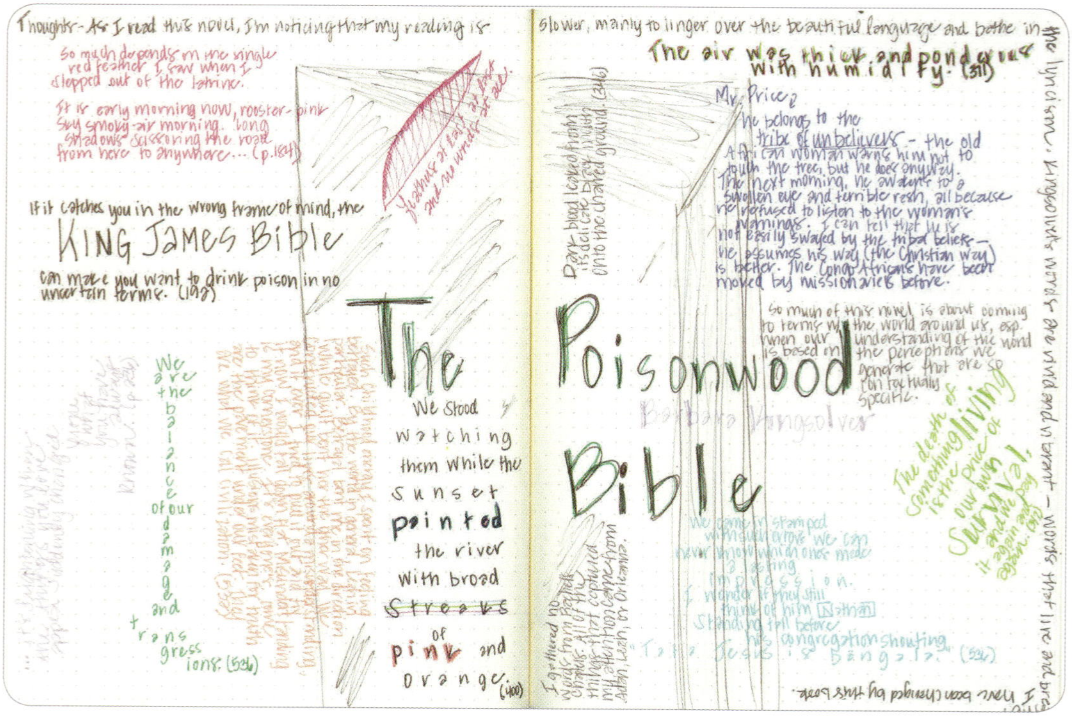

Children need to see possibility. They need to know that creative responses to texts help them unlock ideas that live beneath the text's surface, and the surface of initial response.

I place the entry under the document camera. I say:

"I can't get this novel out of my mind. Take a look at what I've written. I don't do it all in one sitting. I return to the novel several times to see if I can stretch my thinking. Most often, I notice words and phrases that I missed, and I add them to my collection of words, phrases, and sentences."

I tell them to take a few moments to consider:

- What types of sentences did I collect?
- Did I favor one narrator over another?
- What unites the ideas in these sentences?
- What do these sentences tell me about the novel?
- What do they tell me about myself and the types of things I notice when I read?

After students have had some time to study my writing, I talk about the parts of Kingsolver's narrative that resonated with me. I share that when I write and then revisit a notebook entry, I too think about all the questions I have asked them to consider. The questions further my thinking about this, or any, novel.

Then I ask them, "Do you think you could do something like this inside your notebooks?" Some are excited and some are hesitant, but overall, they agree that they want to try. "Yes, we think we can," most of them say. And so we get started.

Management TIP

Students' journal entries are sparked by many moments in the classroom, some planned, some not. Mini-lessons, read-alouds, book conversations between you and students, and peer work all serve as natural jumping-off points for reflection. Probably the most powerful instigator is when I check in with a reader, and sense from the student's words and what is written so far that this learner is poised to make a leap forward in analytical thinking or has the fortitude to tackle something challenging. I then pose a question or suggest to the reader that he or she write about this idea further. Overall, these notebooks are students', not mine. They reside more in the zones of readers' lives than the zone of school. If readers don't value them and their purpose, then their usefulness as a learning tool wanes. So what can teachers do from the start to make them high value? Use them flexibly while embedding them in some consistent routines.

Wrap Up

After giving students a tour of my notebook, I ask them to tell me what they notice. Every year, students talk about how much my artwork adds, how I allow my thinking to become visible inside my notebook, and how I seem to have a very healthy reading life. Perhaps they don't tell me in those exact words, but ultimately, that's what they're getting at. I read and find ways to express myself in my notebook. That helps to inspire them and their notebooks. I tell them I want them to find ways to make the notebooks their very own. I say, "Create something that you would not want to part with. Allow this notebook to become an extension of your soul, a living entity with reactions, responses, and reflections about your reading life and the things inspired by it." What you will find is that your artwork, writing, or whatever it is that shines for them, winds up in their notebooks—but never the same as yours, always theirs.

> Allow this notebook to become an extension of your soul, a living entity with reactions, responses, and reflections about your reading life and the things inspired by it.

Allowing time for working in our notebooks is critical to students developing a process for responding to texts. Students need to see what a fun, engaging habit it is, and to discover the possibilities it offers. And so throughout the first few weeks of school, and even across the entire year, I put my notebook under the document camera, working beside students as they craft, decorate, and prepare to write. I am not the first to say this and I won't be the last, but children today are so scheduled, and so wired, that it's critical for us to build in time for drawing and doodling, as a part of thinking. They reap the benefits of it as "downtime," but it's uptime for their soul.

WE DO Personalizing Notebooks

Students are eager to decorate their notebooks and some students are anxious to start writing inside them. I give kids time to decorate the outside with images, quotes, lyrics, and whatever else they find meaningful. A notebook is a precious thing and ownership of the notebook helps ensure that students will take the work inside it seriously. Linda Rief's *Read Write Teach* (2014) has given my students and me so much inspiration for creating notebooks.

We spend an entire class period working on these notebooks, dividing the books into sections and labeling them. I demonstrate how to maximize writing space by writing from red line to red line, and also by not starting a brand new page for each entry; instead, simply draw a line underneath what you last wrote and write your new entry there. We date and title what we put in our notebooks so when we return to older entries to reflect, it's easier to reconnect to them.

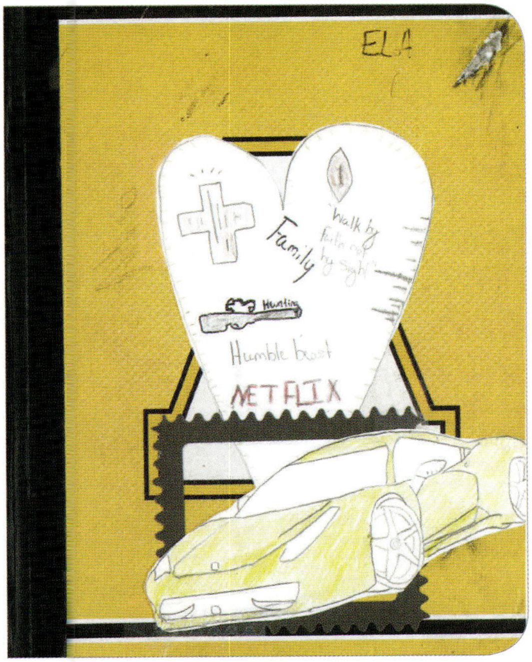

The use of Georgia Heard's heartmaps concept is a favorite with students.

YOU DO Students Do Their First Writing

Early in the week, I may ask students to think and write about their books in their reading response sections. Good teaching is never rushed (Newkirk, 2012), and as students return to school after a weekend, they need to re-establish their reading-thinking minds. Because I place such value on this connection with books, I set aside time for kids to write about their reading. They may choose to write about ideas involving:

- Characters
- Events (plot)
- Predictions
- Things that surprise them
- Questions and/or concerns

Throughout the week, though usually on Mondays, I put what I've been writing under the document camera. Students learn best when they see a process. The final product is not the point; the process is. I may show students a piece of writing connected to a book I'm reading, a blog post I'm working on, or notebook work

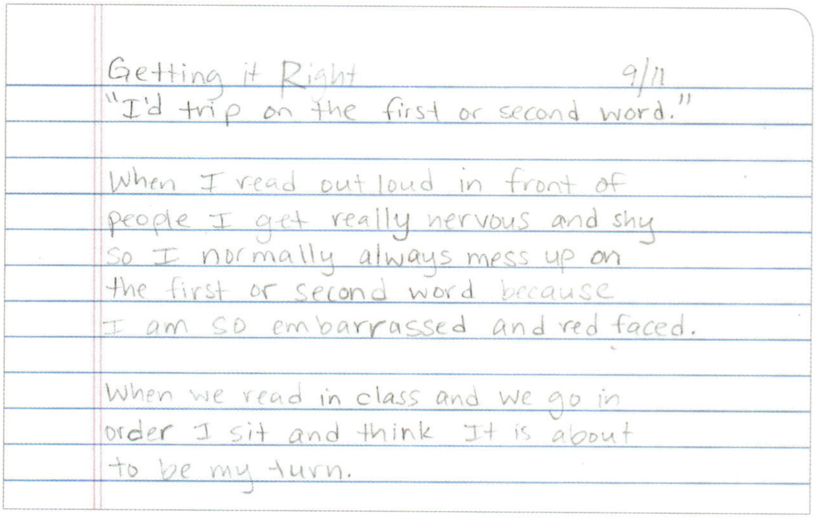
Getting it Right 9/11
"I'd trip on the first or second word."

When I read out loud in front of people I get really nervous and shy so I normally always mess up on the first or second word because I am so embarrassed and red faced.

When we read in class and we go in order I sit and think It is about to be my turn.

Inspired by a piece in Linda Rief's *The Quickwrite Handbook* (2018), Mackenzie wrote of her fear of tripping up on words while reading aloud. She developed this response into a reflection.

inspired by the book I'm currently reading. I show this to them and even give them time across the week to work inside their notebooks on something of their choice.

Scaffolding and Supporting Independence

If I see students struggling, I pull a small group of kids together to discuss a skill or concept that is eluding them. I give them time to ask questions and talk before we do anything instructional. Poems are great texts to use for these shared experiences, but stories, excerpts, and read-alouds work well, too.

> There are often more ideas hidden underneath the ones students write. Show them the intersections in their responses where more thinking might be hiding.

Honoring Students' Unique Needs & Preferences

Part of the joy of a Reader's Workshop is matching kids with books and giving them space and time to read them. One of the hazards, though, can be a tendency to require all reflections be captured in the form of writing. I ask students to jot down their reflections to make the thinking visible, not to create more work. I want it to flow naturally, to pour from their hearts, letting their pencils find the thinking. To help nourish it as a habit for students, not school, I encourage you to set up spaces in your room where kids can talk about their reflections, giving the work a social dimension, much as adults so often do. At the same time, recognize that students at different times want solitude, and may just need to sit with their reflections and hold them in their minds. Go with what feels natural.

YOU DO Friday Reflection

Students reflect on their weekly reading each Friday. If we are still learning about reflective tools—including hashtags, Tweets, and freewrites—I may choose one for them to use, but when they are ready, I release the power of choice to them.

Write About Your Book, Using a Tweet, hashtags, or freewrites (draw on your wonderings, emotions, new thinking . . .)

On Fridays, when students look at what they wrote about their reading and recall conversations, let them then share ideas before they write a new reflection.

Management TIP

Take up notebooks for a single class every other week unless you have a manageable amount of students. If students know you will be looking at their entries and they have a strong foundation in reflective thinking (explicit instruction, models, and an anchor chart), they will think deeply about their books. Have them place a self-stick note on that week's reflection, and possibly the previous week's, so you can track their progress.

 |

I DO Modeling the Various Sparks for Writing

As teachers, we have to hold ourselves to the same expectations we hold our students. Students today are eager for role models of literate living. If we are viewed as "authorities" and arbiters of grades, our students lose out on seeing a mentor read and write and reflect. In my own reading life, I see evidence of change when I sit with an idea that reading stirred, and write in my notebook, and so that is why I share it with students.

Remember, though, that the sparks for writing can be as simple as adding a new word to one's collection of beautiful language.

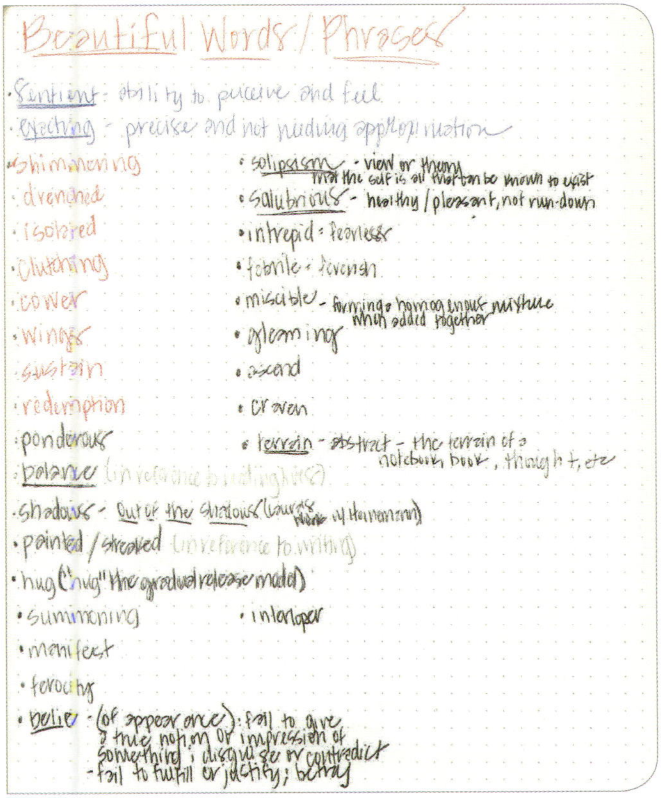

Language is an infectious agent—share it so students "catch" the love of it too.

Why There Are No Short Cuts

When I mention my work with reflection to other educators, some will respond enthusiastically, and say they have been doing this for years. Some will recommend resources or generously forward me links with handouts or printables, always with the implicit message of saving me time. While I appreciate the gestures, and know that reflection isn't a new practice that I invented, I also know that these ready-made resources always die on the vine. Why? Two reasons. The first is that the material is focused on reading response, and not its more complicated, interesting, and moody cousin, reflection. Second, anything that one photocopies and then hands out to students, no matter how authentic it was for the educator who created it, doesn't transplant well into the ecosystem of another classroom. Like a plant indigenous to another soil and climate, these products fail to thrive. That's why this book shares processes, not products.

Students have notebooks, I thought to myself. That's where the ideas need to rise up, not from a handout.

Giving In to Temptation

Even handouts developed by teachers for their students have a static quality that make "live" events of showing process always the better move. A case in point: Not long ago, I was writing in my notebook about an author's use of verbs and metaphor, and began arranging my thoughts into a poem. Inspired, and thinking students would love this same thing, I began creating a handout for them to use. However, I quickly stopped. Students have notebooks, I thought to myself. That's where the ideas need to rise up, not from a handout. So I decided to model what I was doing, and leave it to them to consider it, but then create what works for them inside those notebooks. Brief modeling develops bonds with students because they see all the trial and error of getting ideas on the page. How brief is brief? Two minutes can be potent; try not to go over five minutes.

I DO Learning to Sit with Your Thoughts

In a subsequent lesson, get across that not all reflection needs to—or can—lead to deep levels of thinking in one sitting. Sometimes we just want to sit with the ideas in a book for a while.

I'd like to recount an exchange I had with students not long ago. "Some books stir us to experience beauty," I said. "It's important for you to notice when you are having a reaction to the language or another element of a story. Characters, words, descriptions, or an event might mesmerize you and make you feel something deep inside. That's your heart telling you to slow down and pay attention. Let me tell you about something I experienced recently with a book.

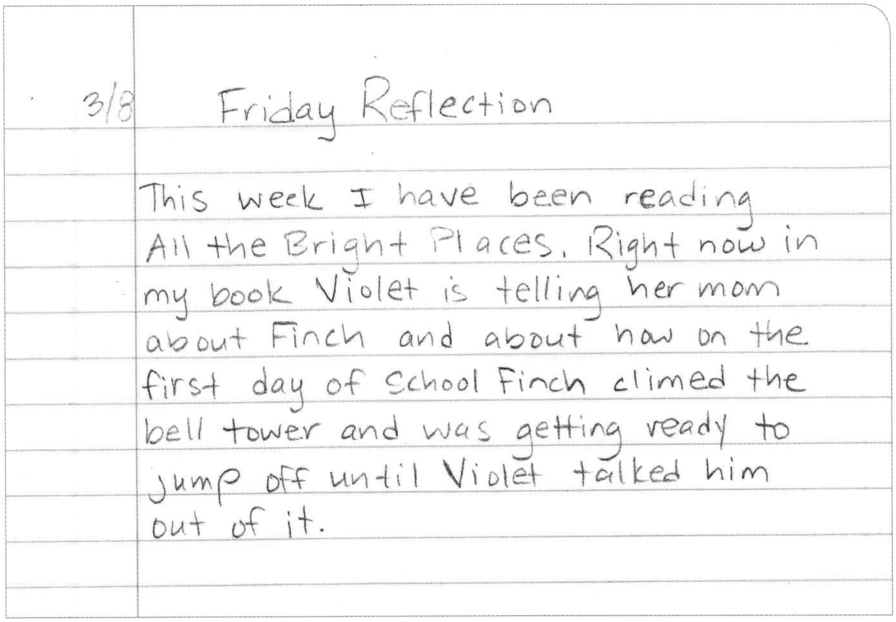
3/8 Friday Reflection

This week I have been reading All the Bright Places. Right now in my book Violet is telling her mom about Finch and about how on the first day of School Finch climed the bell tower and was getting ready to jump off until Violet talked him out of it.

MacKenzie used her writing time to express how much she is enjoying her book.

"When I read *Between Two Skies* by Joanne O'Sullivan, one of the things I noticed immediately was the use of beautiful language and descriptions. Let me show you what I mean." Here, I project an excerpt to show them the beautiful language I noticed. "I kept asking myself, 'How can I emulate these beautiful sentences in my own writing?' O'Sullivan's sentences create vivid images, and I envy her ability to craft amazing phrases. The story of the book deepened my understanding, identity, and belonging, but it was the language that swept me away."

***Between Two Skies* excerpt:**

The next day is my idea of a perfect day. I leave home with Daddy at safe light, going out into the marsh in the Evangeline, gliding up the channels between the canebrakes. There's no noise except the sound of the outboard and just a little rustle of the wind and the water through the tall grass. The light in the east filters up slowly, like the petals of a flower opening, and the shadows take shape.

I put my reflection under the document camera, and point out where I left off. I say to students, "Notice how I lean in to questioning how the writer achieved this in her work? I also wonder if a Quickwrite will help. My thinking on these matters needs time to grow. Some of these ideas landed inside my notebook, but I will return to them."

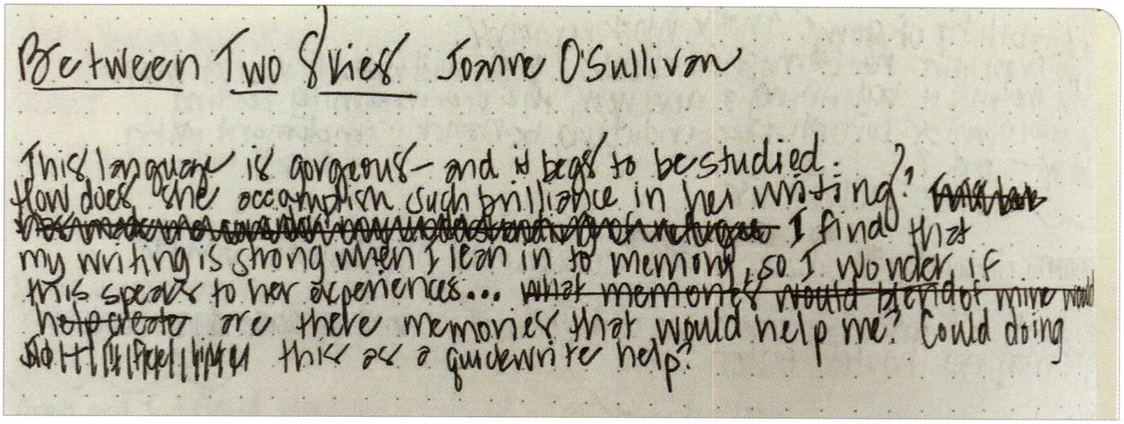
Between Two Skies Joanne O'Sullivan

This language is gorgeous—and it begs to be studied. How does she accomplish such brilliance in her writing? I find that my writing is strong when I lean in to memory, so I wonder if this speaks to her experiences... are there memories that would help me? Could doing this as a quickwrite help?

 |

I wrap up the mini-lesson by encouraging students who never feel compelled to take the time and space to sit with their thoughts. We need this same time and space in our classrooms, because when it's there, remarkable transformation occurs for readers.

When Teaching Nonfiction

As students move through their academic careers, the preponderance of their reading lives will consist of nonfiction. Additionally, students will continue to write mostly nonfiction as they advance from grade to grade. Authors of nonfiction craft sentences and use words to convey meaning to an audience, just like authors of fiction do. I love using pieces from Rick Reilly, Pulitzer-Prize recipient Leonard Pitts Jr., and Cynthia Rylant to demonstrate to students how gorgeous language exists in nonfiction. Jane Yolen and Jason Stemple's nature poems and photographs fuse science and art beautifully. We are in a golden era of nonfiction, and nonfiction today has both literary power but also graphics and visuals to support readers. Make nonfiction a part of your classroom library, and showcase its craft structures to open up possibilities for students' writing, reading, and reflection.

Management TIP

In the beginning, the Workshop process may feel wobbly as you get your footing, but students take to it naturally because it's authentic work. Before too long you will see students making connections, thinking about texts, dropping their thinking in their Reader's Notebooks, and talking with peers and you about the books they're reading. The best advice I can give you is don't think there is a perfect sequence, or that any of these routines are set in stone. Instead, use all the ideas as a springboard to create the workshop flow that works for your students. Lean in and listen to them. They'll tell you where you need to go.

Portrait Gallery of Student Growth

Laura

Beginning-of-the-Year Reflection

Book: *Moo* **by Sharon Creech**

My first impression of this character was that she was somebody that I probably wouldn't want to hang out with since she is from the city but as I've read through the book I have noticed that she is fierce and somebody that could possibly become my friend but she also doesn't really stick with what she's trying to do.

My Take: *Laura has written more of a response, not a reflection. Although she moves into some reflective territory (I notice…), she is still lingering in response, focusing on her impressions the character.*

TRY THIS

When any student, like Laura, needs additional support to reflect, I take a minute or two during independent reading to check in. I'm in essence asking questions that make it safe for them to go beyond in some way. For example, it might be to go beyond in terms of exploring how one's connection to a main character affects the actual reading process. Does this main character's experience affect the way you read this book? Is a character like this causing you to gloss over scenes because she/he is not like you? Or do you find yourself slowing down to try to find common ground? Or, I might ask questions that push the reader to go beyond in terms of generalizing one experience to another. For example: Are you noticing that you are drawn to characters who possess these same qualities?

End-of-the-Year Reflection

Book: ***Shout*** **by Laurie Halse Anderson**

Laurie's dad is falling apart again after doing pretty good but now he's drinking again and is pulling his family's life out of orbit and Laurie prays and cries for him every day. Laurie is going from school to school talking about her book *Speak* which also talks about rape and everybody who she talks to is saying that her book is "inappropriate" and she's struggling to understand why because she feels by not teaching kids early about rape and things relating to that, it's only protecting the adult. I agree with Laurie. *Shout* made me cringe, but it made me realize the importance of listening to people, not just assuming they are telling a lie. This showed me that it's important to respect victims and listen to people who have had something like this done to them. They deserve to be heard.

My Take: *Laura begins her reflection as response, but she moves into reflection when she began explaining what this book has shown her and what she has realized since reading* Shout *by Laurie Halse Anderson. It's not just the length of the reflection but the depth that separates this one from her reflection earlier in the year.*

TRY THIS

When students arrive at thinking such as this, the profound nature of the thinking should be celebrated. Assumptions drive our reactions, but when young people notice how wrong their assumptions can be, it is worthy of praise. Additionally, I would recommend more reading. *Blood Water Paint* **by Joy McCullough is a gorgeous novel-in-verse, written about a woman who speaks her truth in Rome in the 1600s and is encouraged to remain silent in the male-dominated society. I would also encourage writing here— how does it feel to know something is true but not be believed?**

A Reflection

Since reading *1984*, I've noticed that other texts are easier to understand. There were words that were difficult to understand, but I looked them up online, and now I'm even using them in my writing. Winston's character was interesting and during check-ins, I began to notice how relevant this book is. I've never read a book quite like this one, and I'm not sure if I understood everything in it, but I understood most of it. Reading it again would probably help. I would like to read the opening chapter again.

—Makenna, 8th grade student

Concluding Thoughts: Faith

In this chapter, the following points have been explored:

- The Reader's Notebook is a place where students house their thinking and it is the place where you can get inside their heads and understand how to help them as readers and thinkers.
- Notebooks belong to the students. If they don't own them, they won't work. Students have to "wear them in," so to speak, by personalizing them and writing inside them.
- It is essential that you keep a notebook, too. This can't be one that you use just for class; it has to belong to you and must be something that holds your responses and reflections about your reading life.

Consider this moment in my classroom: Rays of sun landed in parallel bars, decorating the carpet and the backs of students who lay there with light as they read. Clipboard in hand, ready to begin check-ins, I noticed that students were so immersed in their books. I hesitated, and watched them a moment. This particular group of students had experienced a tenuous journey with independent reading, but now, after months of consistent nudging, each of them found a way to love books.

> Make sure your students are aware of the craft of nonfiction writing, too. It has the power to stir us as well.

 |

The sounds of reading—turning pages and relaxed breathing—mesmerized me. I decided to engage just a couple of students in conversation. I spoke with Faith, a student whose inability to settle into a reading life had caused her frustration since the beginning of the year. She could not find a book that resonated with her. But a few weeks ago, she picked *Orbiting Jupiter* by Gary Schmidt off the shelf. Others in the class had enjoyed the book, and so she gave it a try. I had watched her as she started.

Cultivating a love for reading is one of the most important things we do as teachers.

QUESTIONS *to* ASK YOURSELF

- **Do you keep a notebook? If so, how does your notebook help you navigate and more deeply understand the books you read? If not, how might your reading life change if you had one?**
- **Read for 15-20 minutes and jot down examples of language that grabs you. What do you notice about this language? Why did it stand out to you? How might your own noticings help your students as readers and thinkers?**
- **If you don't already, how could you schedule time for students to personalize their own notebooks to establish ownership? How could you modify and adapt your own so students can see that you, too, are participating in this process?**

She didn't move her eyes from the pages for the entire reading time. She had even hid the book under her desk and read it during a mini-lesson, but I sure wasn't going to bust her for doing that.

On this day, Faith was lost in *Three Black Swans* by Caroline B. Cooney. I was curious about how it was going for Faith. I approached her and a smile spread across her face. I asked her to tell me what she was thinking about as she read, and after hearing several of her ideas, I smiled and asked, "What made you realize that you could love reading?" She responded, "Because I found a book that made me think."

> That is the ultimate goal I have for all of my students. Faith found a book that moved her to reflect, and from there she realized that books about tough issues, especially ones related to foster children, were of interest to her.

Reflective thinking gives students the opportunity to discover their reading interests and habits. This is what it means to develop a reading identity. There is no official format, worksheet, or formulaic writing assignment that can engage students in this type of deep reflective thinking. I use tools such as questions and conversations to help children negotiate their thinking and mold it into richer thoughts, but they are only vehicles to move students to reflect. Time and space to read, write, and think are the essential pieces.

Space and time are key ingredients in the process of students unlocking their reading identities.

Further Reading

Here are some of my favorite professional texts that include materials and resources related to the importance and value of a Reader's Notebook:

Inside the Writer's-Reader's Notebook
by Linda Rief

That Workshop Book
by Samantha Bennett

In the Middle
by Nancie Atwell

And here are some favorite literary works:

The Soul of an Octopus
by Sy Montgomery

Internment
by Samira Ahmed

The Whispers
by Greg Howard

Between Shades of Gray
by Ruta Sepetys

The Book Thief
by Markus Zusak

American Street
by Ibi Zoboi

The Astonishing Color of After
by Emily X.R. Pan

Caraval
by Stephanie Garber

Hurricane Season
by Nicole Melleby

The Benefits of Being an Octopus
by Ann Braden

How is Reflection like a Map?
Provides clarity
Where am I?
Show us where to go!
Provides understanding
Provides direction
DATE
SUBJECT
READ
STUDY
CRAFT
SHARE
Writing
Part I:
FRONT DESK
THE WHISPERS
CHILDREN OF BLOOD AND BONE
THE POET X
DUMPLIN'

CHAPTER 4

Discovering Your Readers

Most students come into my classroom with little experience in reflective thinking. This metacognitive act is critical for any learner of any age. We grow because we grapple with our thinking. My students' lack of experience is not a negative thing; embracing challenge, growth, and change is learning. It means that as teachers, we need to embrace classroom structures that are decidedly simple, for there is power in simplicity.

> We need to embrace classroom structures that are decidedly simple, for there is power in simplicity.
>
> ***S. Travis Crowder***

In this chapter, I provide best practice strategies and tools that will help you get to know your readers. This initial work of discovering readers' interests and habits of thinking prepares them for the activities I discuss in chapter 5—such as Tweets, hashtags, and freewrites—which invite students to elaborate more, trust more, and engage more.

You'll want to use these tools collaboratively, so students use them on their own and inch closer to independent reflective reading habits.

Interest Inventories

To nudge students in their reading lives and to begin to know who they are, I begin the year with interest inventories, which give them a chance to write about the things they love. On beginning-of-the-year inventories, I ask questions such as:

- What is a book you've read and loved?
- How would you describe yourself as a reader?
- What challenges do you face as a reader?
- What genres do you enjoy?
- What is your favorite movie?
- What is your favorite song?
- Are you an athlete? What types of sports do you play?
- What do you enjoy doing in your spare time?

Students' interests may not match their personalities. Inventories help you discover their preferences.

Management TIP

Students return to their inventories in the middle of the year and at the end of the year to determine how they've grown. In Chapter 5, I give a detailed assessment for students to use to help them make sense of their growth as readers. Their understanding of their growth and changes as readers helps inform this larger, more in-depth self-assessment at the end of the year.

Learning from Students

I collect students' responses and review them before they come back to class the following day. These inventories go in their portfolios, and students revisit them a few times during the school year. Sometimes, I ask them to update their answers; other times, I ask them to consider how they have changed since they first encountered the inventory. Students are very often surprised by their changes as readers and thinkers throughout a school year.

Reading & Interest Inventory

Name ______________________________ Date ______________

1. What is a book you have read and loved? What made that book so wonderful? (Try to give the title and the author.)

2. Do you like to read? Why or why not?

3. Which of the following genres are you usually interested in? Circle all that apply.

a.	realistic fiction	b.	historical fiction	c.	poetry
d.	graphic novels	e.	biography	f.	autobiography/ memoir
g.	informational books	h.	fantasy	i.	science fiction
j.	dystopian	k.	horror	l.	mystery/thriller
m.	adventure	n.	picture books	o.	comedy/humor

4. Of the genres listed above, which one(s) do you think you would like to read first this year?

5. In your opinion, what makes someone a reader?

6. What is a goal you have for yourself as a reader?

7. What do you love to do in your spare time?

Conversation

Conversation is another important tool when we think about getting to know our students. Readers talk, and through that conversation, they learn how to use and navigate readerly language—words and phrases that readers use to discuss books and stories.

I start conversations with students on the first day of school, interacting with them as they complete their interest inventories. I listen for language that will give me a glimpse of their true selves because we will spend an entire year reading together. Usually, their interests inform their reading lives, so I need to know if they are athletes, musicians, introverts, extroverts, readers, lovers of film, and so on. Knowing this information guides me as I match them with books. These initial conversations ground my work with students for the remainder of the year because we talk constantly, especially about books and stories.

Discovering the kinds of books and topics students gravitate toward is a great first step in a year of reading and learning together.

Supporting Zachary

At the beginning of this school year, I sat beside Zachary as he responded to the questions on the interest survey.

Me: So, Zachary, tell me about you.

Zachary: Well, what would you like to know?

Me: What sorts of things do you like to read?

Zachary: I don't really read. I prefer to stay active.

Me: Ok. Have you ever read a book you really enjoyed?

Zachary: Yeah . . . um . . . I really liked *The Crossover* by . . . I can't remember—

Me: Kwame Alexander.

Zachary: Yeah, him, and I really liked how it was about basketball. That was one of the first books I read last year. It was also one of the best.

Me: How many books did you read last year?

Zachary: Um . . . about 20, maybe? 25?

Me: Wow! That's a pretty big number for someone who says he doesn't like to read.

Zachary: Well, I do like stories, but given the option I would prefer to be active.

Me: So you do read, you just find yourself choosing athletics over books.

Zachary: Yeah, I guess you could say that.

Me: You know, lots of readers do that. You might surprise yourself a lot this year. You may find a book that you can't get enough of.

Zachary: Maybe.

Shifting a Reader's Self-Concept

During this quick, informal conversation with Zachary, I invited him to reflect on his past reading experiences and think about the decisions he might make as a reader this school year. As we spoke, I learned quite a bit about his reading habits. For a supposed non-reader, he read more than 20 books in the previous year. In this conversation, I wanted him to own that accomplishment. If he did indeed read over 20 books (he did because I checked with his English teacher), he had had a successful year as a reader.

From this exchange, I was able to help Zachary realize he is a reader by changing his concept of what a "reader" is. He came in with an idea that a real "reader" is someone who chooses to read before doing anything else. I assured Zachary that "readers" can read books and participate in other activities, a concept I hope he carries with him beyond our class.

Reflective thinking takes trusting oneself and one's teacher, and maintaining ongoing dialogue.

Responding to Questions

With each student, I use the inventories and follow-up questions to both break the ice and speed the pace of meeting their needs. It ought not take us weeks to discover who they are; it should take days. While skimming those inventories, I'm already scheming about which books or authors they might love and choosing what new graphic novels are going to be in my Amazon Prime cart by sundown.

And as is true in the beginning of any relationship, questions and responses- even when they seem a bit formal at first- scaffold familiarity. Similarly, questions provide students with a scaffold as they are getting used to opening up to reflective thinking.

> . . . "readers" can read books and participate in other activities, a concept I hope he carries with him beyond our class.

Each Friday, at the end of class, I ask students to think about their reading lives across the week and write their thinking in their reading response sections. (See page 72 in previous chapter.) We each look back at our reading experiences and write about our reading. In the beginning of the year, students often do this work in response to questions. Just pose a few at a time from which they can choose.

Some questions you might pose to students

- What did you notice about yourself as a reader this week?
- Are you enjoying this book? Why or why not?
- How is this book matching your interests as a reader?
- Are you finding that you are connecting with the main character? Why or why not?
- Would you be the main character's best friend? Explain your answer.
- Are you independent enough to select your own books using your to-read list and the recommendations of your teacher and classmates? How so?
- How many pages did you read this week? How do you feel about that number of pages?
- What goal did you set last week? Did you meet it? What challenges stood in your way?
- Write about your reading life this week. What parts of your book have you enjoyed? What surprised you in your reading? What were the challenges you experienced? How did you overcome them? How have you changed as a reader since the beginning of the year?
- Has your thinking changed—about characters, the plot, the big ideas or themes—since you started reading this book? How so?

> Although inquisitiveness is natural in children, we nonetheless have to cultivate–and model–what we mean by having a questioning, reflective mindset.

Other times you might pose these questions

Sometimes I ask one or two of these questions during individual reading conversations with students; other times, I ask one of the questions and students respond in their reader's notebooks. Students are constantly responding to their reading through summarizing, writing about characters, and exploring big ideas.

Bigger reflective questions to pose

When I sense students are ready for bigger reflective thinking, I give them each a sticky note and ask them reflective questions that surround smaller questions. For example, if students write about a character, describing that character's fears, personality, and relationships (smaller question), I may ask them, "Would you be this character's best friend? Why or why not?" (bigger question). They would then write this bigger reflective question on the sticky note and place it on the characterization entry they made inside their notebooks.

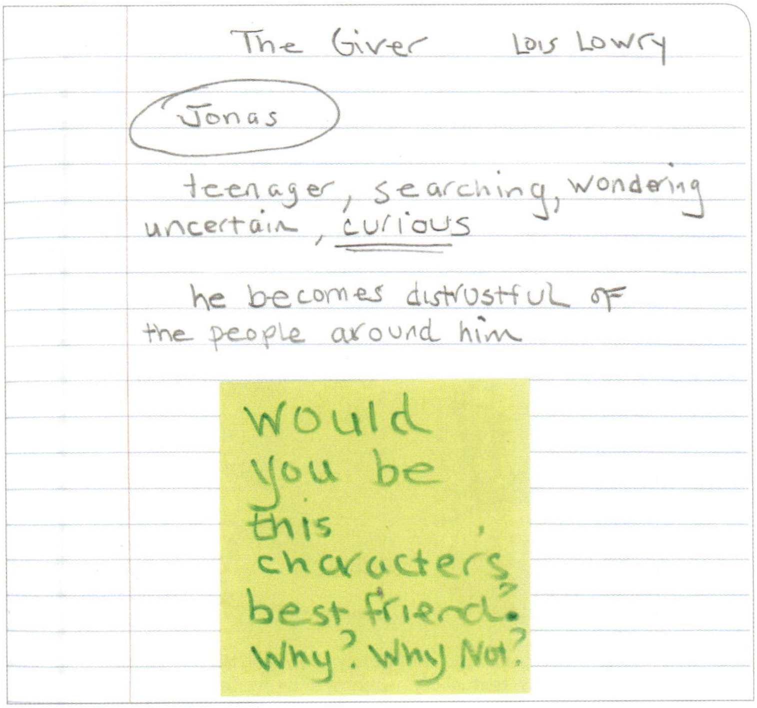

Pose questions that invite a reader to elaborate and go deeper with their thinking.

Other bigger reflective questions to be answered on sticky notes may include:

- Is this a big idea or theme you have read quite a bit this year? Why do you feel attracted to this big idea/theme?
- Are you regularly meeting/not meeting your reading goals? What challenges are you overcoming/not overcoming?
- How has your independence as a reader changed from last year to this year?

I try to limit the amount of sticky notes I give students across the year because they can take over a student's notebook; however, asking these larger questions every so often helps students push their thinking about their reading lives, especially the decisions they are making as readers.

The beauty of reflective thinking is that it isn't purely analytical. It's a blend of logic, aesthetics, personal connections, textual connections, and reverie.

How Kids Articulate the Benefits

When I was writing this book, I asked my students how they perceived the benefits of questions and reflective thinking:

Amelia explained to me that the reflective process gave her time to assess herself and see big ideas across the texts she read independently, as well as short stories and poems we read together as a class. She also noted that she was not leaning on my opinion, but instead was expected to develop her own ideas about herself and about her growth as a reader.

> . . . asking these larger questions every so often helps students push their thinking about their reading lives, especially the decisions they are making as readers.

Harris told me that after reflecting across several weeks, he began cementing his thinking about how reading relates to real life.

Pedro said that reflections in class made him think and track his progress as a reader because he could see the trail of thinking in his notebook.

All of these students talked about adjustments that they made to their reading habits and their thinking because of the reflection—through conversation and writing—they completed in class.

Portrait Gallery of Student Growth

Emma-Kate

Beginning-of-the-Year Reflection

Book: ***Amal Unbound*** **by Aisha Saeed**

I got this book Monday & I've read ~~eighty-three~~ 83 pages this week but it's because this book isn't really ~~good~~ intriguing. ~~I mean~~ it's not terrible but it's not the best I've read. I'm just now getting into a good part.

My Take: *Notice how Emma-Kate edited to meet a 240-character limit. This reflection shows the truth about our reading lives—sometimes our reactions to texts are not always positive. Weaving the honesty of reading into this Tweet helps Emma-Kate see growth over time.*

TRY THIS

For Emma-Kate and any other student who isn't enjoying a book, I want to discover what about a book is not working for them. More important, I want to confer so that the student knows that. Sometimes a quick trip to the book shelf to survey other genres inspires students' thinking about what might be a new genre to try. Talking about authors, titles, genres, back cover descriptions as we physically flip through books helps the student and me converse.

Middle-of-the-Year Reflection

Book: *To Kill a Mockingbird* by Harper Lee and
Insignificant Events in the Life of a Cactus by Dusti Bowling

I am so proud of myself because I've read 130 pages this week & I finished To Kill a Mockingbird & am already almost finished with Insignificant Events in the Life of a Cactus. I have noticed that sometimes I have to go back and re-read things that I was like "wait what was that" and I've also noticed some books I read SUPER FAST and some I read SLOWER.

My Take: *Here, Emma-Kate is noticing her reading process and her pace. She recognizes the value of re-reading and recognizing how the type of book affects her pace. The Tweets show a change in her thinking—she has pinpointed the moments when she is reading more slowly, noticed how her interest matches the pace of her reading, and gave herself permission to read parts again to deepen her comprehension.*

TRY THIS

I want Emma-Kate to push her self-reflection about her reading life. I'd pose questions like: What has changed from the beginning of the year? Is there a book that helped get your reading underway? How is your thinking now different? The most important thing to me is that I see readers flourish, and in their notebooks see that they are basking in the beauty of the story. Yet I also expect them to be able to speak to the things that helped them grow into their stronger reading lives.

Questions for the Entire Reading Process

Before, during, and after reading—these are the familiar, unimpeachable three-phases of text engagement that we talk about as educators. Put them together and they become "the entire reading process." In reality, the borders are blurred like chalk drawings after rain, but no matter. The point is, questions authentically bubble up throughout, whether we are aware of them or not. Something gets stirred in our minds, and maybe not quite answered enough. It can be all sorts of wonderings: Is this novel set in an actual town? Is the main character like the author? Why did that scene make me so sad? Why did the people in colonial America die younger than we do today? Although inquisitiveness is natural in children, we nonetheless have to cultivate—and model—what we mean by having a questioning, reflective mindset. This is where having a big store of questions comes in handy; it is starter fluid you might use before, during, and after reading, as needed.

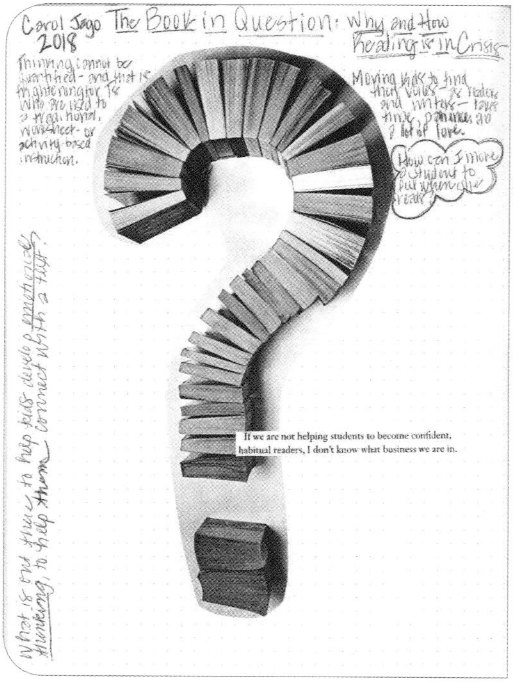

Like signs on a highway, questions provide a reader with a way to navigate thinking as they interact with text.

Questions Before Reading

In the classroom, and not unlike when sampling novels in an aisle of a bookstore, before-reading questions flicker as a way to help us choose what to read. A peer's recommendations are powerful, but I still think students benefit from teachers thinking aloud their book selection habits. Use the following questions as the springboard for mini-lessons on book choice, and invite students to answer these questions in talks or in their notebooks.

- What are you looking for in a book? Is there a type of character or a particular idea that you're drawn to?
- What's on your To-Read list?
- Where are you in your reading life? What do you feel would be a good next step as a reader?
- What type of book—genre, format, or author—might be a step outside of your comfort zone?
- How did your last book challenge you? Are you ready for one that will push you as a thinker and reader?
- In your notebook, you've written a lot about the books and texts you've read in class. What do you notice you've written about most? Is that something you'd like to continue reading about?

I still think students benefit from teachers thinking aloud their book selection habits.

Questions During Reading

I use questions often to help kids make sense of their reading. I ask students to write these questions down in their notebooks, or sometimes, paste photocopies of them inside their notebooks.

- How is this book matching your interests?
- What are you noticing as you read, either about the text or yourself?
- What surprises you?
- What story is this author trying to tell with this book?
- What do the problems tell you about the character?
- What argument do you feel this author is trying to make? What words stand out to you?
- Is there something the author is implying but isn't directly stating? What might that message be?

What viewpoints or narratives do you think are missing from this text? Is there a text that possesses it? If not, let's look together for a text that will let us hear these voices.

Management TIP

Reflections are powerful formative assessment data. I prefer to use student reflections as indicators of progress instead of antiseptic numbers and data points. For me, conversations and narratives are authentic. They let me peer into the minds and hearts of children, a guide to the continued work I will do with them during the school year.

Questions for After Finishing a Book

As much as teachers should encourage reading volume, we want to cultivate students' capacity to "sit still" after finishing a book. I liken this moment of reflection to when you have just watched a powerful movie in a theater; after its ending, you just sit there watching the credits roll and listening to the ending score, glad for the lights staying dimmed, so you can keep taking in what you have just experienced. While our cultural habit may be to wipe our tears and collect ourselves so other movie goers don't see what an emotional mess we are, a powerful movie will continue to disrupt and upset us constructively in the days and weeks that follow. Whether it's a love story, war story, or story of human suffering, it changes us and may compel us to act.

With students, then, my goal for posing questions after they have finished the book is to help them unravel the ideas they have, and discover the ones they didn't know were lurking beneath the placid surface of their thinking.

When a student finishes a book, I may ask questions such as:

- What did you think? How is this like other books you've read?
- How has your thinking changed since starting this book?
- How have you changed as a reader because of this book?
- What did you notice—about the text or yourself—as you read this book?
- How has writing about your reading informed your understanding of the book and your journey?
- Now that you've read this book, what are you feeling?
- What do you feel you need to do because of this book?
- Is there a person you feel needs to read this text? If so, who? Can you tell me why?
- When did this book start nudging you as a reader and thinker?
- Do I need to read this book? Why?

Students need time to think as they read and when they finish reading. They can do this by writing, talking about it with a partner, or thinking to themselves.

When Teaching Nonfiction

Creative, engaging nonfiction for elementary and middle school readers abounds. A quick Google search yields many teacher and librarian-curated lists. The Orbis Pictus Awards are akin to the Pulitzer, so stock your classroom library with those winners and honors books, as well as titles for students who express interest in sports, history, current events, and/or celebrities. The *Who Was* book series (www.whowasbookseries.com) may provide students with a helpful start to their reading lives. I also recommend *Undefeated: Jim Thorpe and the Carlisle Indian School Football Team* as a great text for students to read and study. The opening section of the book is an accessible mentor text that shows readers an option for writing narrative nonfiction.

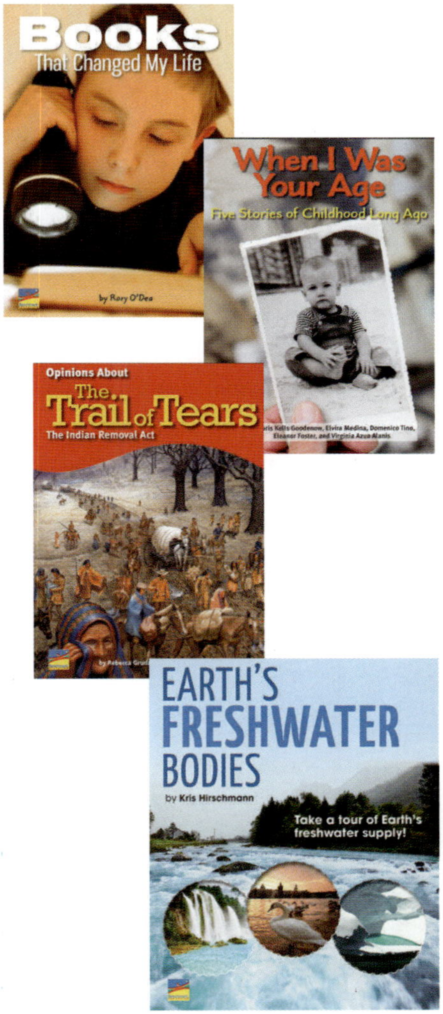

Carrying the Ideas Across the School Year

A confession: Deciding how to organize ideas on reflective reading into chapters is like trying to catch a minnow with bare hands. It's hard to take the complex, ever-darting actions of teaching and make them sit still on a book page. Practical advice about minutes, frequency of routines, and great questions to pose swim to the surface in each chapter where they are needed. Yet as an avid professional book reader, I know that wish to have the basic advice all in one spot. So on the next page, I provide you with The Mega List of Management Tips. Now you have all the book's essential routines in one big fish bowl to gaze at and make your own.

The Mega List of Management TIPS for Reflective Reading

Notebook To-Dos

- Hand out black and white composition notebooks to each student.
- Have kids personalize them.
- Plan on having kids review their entries after a few weeks when they have 5-6 written.
- Check in with each reader at least once a week, usually during independent reading time. It can also be in the hallway, during class change, on the way to lunch, or during some other impromptu time.
- Read reader's notebooks about once every other week.
- Write comments in them to nudge kids as thinkers.

Mini-lesson/Modeling To-Dos

- Deliver a mini-lesson to readers about three times a week, drawing topics from what you notice/standards.
- Use mini-lessons as an opportunity to encourage reading and thinking, as well as to create a reminder of learning (i.e. an anchor chart).
- Put your notebook under the document camera often.
- Model vulnerability by writing "on the fly" in front of students.
- Give students opportunities to put their notebooks under the document camera and share what they've written.

Formative Assessment To-Dos

- Have a place to keep notes about individual students. I use a legal pad to keep track of my notes and have a single sheet, front and back, to record my observations for each student.
- Use the first week of school to observe and make notes about students. What do you notice about them? Do certain behaviors stand out? What books are students selecting? Which ones are they abandoning?
- Note when students are not reading or fake reading. That's your cue to talk with them.
- Keep a list of things students struggle to articulate during check-ins. Use that list to inform the mini-lessons you share with them.

Book Talk To-Dos

- Do a book talk at least twice a week—more if possible.
- Make sure by October your students are doing book talks, too.
- Celebrate reading with students. When they finish a book, let them know you see them.

Display To-Dos

- Keep a reminder of learning in your classroom. Anchor charts from mini-lessons should be displayed throughout the room.
- Display an anchor chart that gives an overview of what reflection is and what it allows readers to do.
- Display an anchor chart that explains what WRITING ABOUT READING is and how students can use Tweets, freewrites, and hashtags to explore their reading.
- Display a list of books that students have read (e.g. as a poster). Make it visible so students can consult it as a way to grow their reading lives and to-read lists in their notebooks.
- Have students write book recommendations on notecards or sticky notes and put those inside the front cover. Put those books on tops of counters, bookshelves, or a ledge under your board.

End-of-Year To-Dos

- Ask students to go through their notebooks and highlight their reflections.
- Use "A Year of Reading Reflections" to help your students unpack their year of reflecting.
- Consider using "A Year of Reading Reflections" for yourself.
- Encourage students to articulate how reflection has helped them as a reader during the school year.
- Make sure you leave them with an understanding of transfer. Discuss how they can take this to the next grade level even if their teachers do not use a system of reflective thinking in their classrooms.

Concluding Thoughts: Discovery

In this chapter, the following points have been explored:

- Interest inventories, conversations, and questions help you get to know the readers in your classroom.
- Responses to the inventories and the information you collect from conversations with students help you understand their reading preferences, as well as who they are and how you can help them find the reading that matters to them.
- Before-reading, during-reading, and after-reading questions help students make sense of their books, and they begin to get a sense of the work readers do when they settle into a reading life.

Our teaching comes alive when we allow each class, each year, to influence our plans.

Getting to know your readers is the most important step in helping them develop a literate life. Discovery helps you, but more importantly, it helps the students understand their reading preferences. Additionally, reading is an inherently social act—we want to talk about the books we read. By asking questions, you are modeling how inquiry helps you get to know someone, and how it helps you make sense of the text you hold in your hands.

Further Reading

The Book Whisperer by Donalyn Miller

Reading in the Wild by Donalyn Miller with Susan Kelly

Mosaic of Thought by Ellin Keene and Susan Zimmermann

Getting to know your readers is the most important step in helping them develop a literate life.

QUESTIONS to ASK YOURSELF

- What role does conversation play in your classroom?
- How can you use interest inventories, one-on-one conversations, and discussions around books to better understand your students?
- How can the data you collect about students through interest inventories and conversations help you tailor your instruction? How can it help you match students with books?

Big Ideas in Texts
·love ·loyalty ·trust
·honesty ·abuse
·mercy ·discrimination

CHAPTER 5

Inviting Reflective Thinking

Students are usually quite adept at responding to their reading. Reflective thinking, though, requires time to cultivate. As Karina commented in one of her check-ins, "Reflection makes me think about what I'm learning. Before this year, I would write what I felt, but now I have to go beyond that." As we saw in the previous chapter, inviting students to answer questions is a way to warm up learners for the heavier lifting that reflective thinking requires. In this chapter, I share ideas that nudge students to think reflectively on their own and to reach for the big ideas, for it's these ideas that make us feel most alive. From the movie *Casablanca* to Kwame Alexander's *The Crossover*, and every story in between, narratives help us connect with the universe's big ideas. From there comes joy, solace, and belonging.

"From the movie *Casablanca* to Kwame Alexander's *The Crossover,* and every story in between, narratives help us to connect with the universe's big ideas. From there come joy, solace, and belonging."

S. Travis Crowder

Using Tweets to Get Started

Tweets, freewrites, and hashtags are three forms I use to help students explore and connect with their reading lives. Let's begin with Twitter which is such a busy universe. In succinct, 240-character updates, we can share moments of thought. When I first started using Twitter I was not fond of it, but then I began to appreciate how Twitter forced me to think differently about language. While participating in a Twitter chat one evening, I was expressing how a book had influenced me, and I noticed how focused I was on syntax, concise language, and word choice—all of the things I attend to when writing any kind of text I care about. It hit me then that using the Twitter constraints could be terrific for my students when writing about their reading. It would be a simple way to teach revision of thinking, too. I wondered if it would alleviate some of the anxiety students naturally feel when faced with an entire blank page.

In succinct, 240-character updates, we can share moments of thought.

Management TIP

Asking for a Tweet-length response helps students get closer to the heart of what they are trying to say. If students choose to use a different tool when they reflect independently, they will have had this great practice in writing succinctly. Your students may complain wildly about the 240-character limit, but it's worth it! I found it really builds their confidence before penning longer reflections.

I DO Considering Character with a Tweet

Clay's Quilt by Silas House is an exceptional mentor text for thinking about character. In this lesson I used the character Clay to show students how my own thinking about this protagonist had evolved. Following are some highlights of the demonstration:

- I grappled with the idea in my notebook, getting my ideas on the page first, then, I revised. The first draft (the first segment beginning "Clay's family has a tendency...") was where my thinking began, but it was well over the 240-character limit.
- Under the document camera, I showed students how I took the first draft and revised it so it would be Tweet-length (see the last notebook entry, shown below). I showed them how I modified the first sentence, used a semicolon to separate and fuse ideas, and changed the word "thought" to "felt," conveying the same idea but letting them know that the word "felt" has a heart connection, the type of emotional thinking I want them to experience in their own reading lives.
- After showing them how I grappled with this Tweet-length reflection, I asked students to try crafting their own reflections, and model them after mine. Then, I sent them to work in their notebooks.

Modeling for students how to whittle a wordy draft into a concise Tweet is an engaging revision lesson.

Supporting Students

This type of writing is an exercise in concision. I've found that most students struggle to put their thoughts into succinct language, so I encourage them to write what they want to say first, and then remove unnecessary words and/or phrases.

Every reader is different, and every student will be at a different place in an independent reading life. Some readers will devour books and will have at their disposal many complex characters to think about as they reflect. These readers have noticed character transformation again and again, and so, more than likely, they are aware of the pattern of change in characters. At the other end of the spectrum are students who are just coming into their reading lives, and they are still grappling with whether they can grow to love reading. There are also readers who are striving to make sense of a text, and their focus is on the events, keeping up with characters, and making meaning of the words on the page. Because I work with readers at various stages in reading development, I am sensitive to the way I frame questions and activities like Tweet-length responses to my students. I work one-on-one with readers who need extra support.

I've found that most students struggle to put their thoughts into succinct language . . .

IDC Modeling Freewriting

I love using nontraditional tools such as Tweets and hashtags to engage students in the process of reflection, but there is something beautiful about the simplicity of a freewrite. Demonstration, as always, is key, as watching and hearing the process helps students unpack the moves of freewriting. I place my notebook under the document camera and think aloud about my own reading—what I've read, what my reading life has included, and what I've gained from this reading experience.

Supporting Students

Thinking aloud during the demonstration process is also vital to students' understanding of how freewrites can help with reflective thinking. I begin with what I'm thinking about as I prepare to write and how my thinking leads to new thinking. I am writing to discover what I want to say.

Demonstration helps students appreciate the value of freewriting. They see how the exercise helps one uncover one's thinking and best ideas.

A Reflection

I'm reading *Where is Alcatraz?* by Nico Medina. I notice that I am liking nonfiction more than I thought I would. The illustrations are good. Alcatraz was a place for criminals but it's closed now. I want to read more about it. I like reading about the escape attempts.

–Ivan, 4th grader

Supporting Students

Students need several laps around the proverbial track with crafting Tweets. Hunched over their notebooks, they will compulsively count each character. They love the challenge. Inviting them into this process is key, though. I do not take a grade on this assignment; I only use it as a springboard for further conversations with each reader. As the year progresses and students grow into their reading lives, I will stretch their thinking by asking more challenging questions. These include:

- What is a big idea in this book, and what evidence in your book supports that?
- What is this novel teaching you about people? Why is this important?
- What is a question the central character is wrestling with? How is that character attempting to answer it?

As the year progresses and students grow into their reading lives, I will stretch their thinking by asking more challenging questions.

 |

I have students who stare at their notebooks for long periods of time and are hesitant to craft a Tweet. Some students will write their thinking, but they will not revise so that it is 240-characters long. I am not frustrated with them, but I do ask them during independent reading conversations to explain why they struggled with the activity. Most of the time, we are able to revise it together, and that gives them strategies to use the next time we reflect using Twitter as a format.

Writing about reading should always feel useful to students. They need to experience it as a help to them, or it becomes just another thing to do for school.

I DO Modeling Vulnerability with an Opening Paragraph

I do not ask students to do something I am unwilling to do. Whenever I ask them to complete a task or try a new strategy in their reading lives, they are taking a risk and stepping outside their current level of comfort and ability. It wasn't until I read *The Art of Slow Reading* by Thomas Newkirk (2012) that I realized the power of deliberately modeling vulnerability as a reader. Newkirk suggests a cold read—demonstrating a reading and interpretation of a text in front of students so they can watch you wrestle with meaning and analysis. Making my struggle as a reader visible changed the dynamic of my classroom; more students were willing to take risks with their interpretations.

Here's what I did with Toni Morrison's novel, *Beloved*. I had read it for the first time several months earlier, and it profoundly affected me as a reader and thinker.

Highlights of the lesson

- I photocopied the first few pages of *Beloved* and positioned the excerpt under the document camera.
- I shared with students how much I had loved reading the book, but that it was a challenging experience because the text is loaded with references, characters, and events that are at first glance confusing.
- I said that even though I slowed down to read and reread, there were still parts that I needed to unpack, and that I wanted to do this work in front of them so they could hear my process.
- I explained to students that I would be demonstrating a think-aloud process for interpreting texts using reflective and analytical thinking to unpack the first few paragraphs of the book.
- And then I began to think aloud...(see next page).

 |

"124 was spiteful. Full of a baby's venom."

So here, I'm starting to get a sense of the feel and the tone that Toni Morrison is setting in this book. "Venom" does not have a positive connotation, so I'm assuming from these first few sentences that there is a sense of fear, and of uncertainty.

"The women in the house knew it and so did the children. For years each put up with the spite in his own way, but by 1873 Sethe and her daughter Denver were its only victims."

It's 1873, so this is after the American Civil War. I'm wondering if the uncertainty is related to an event in the Civil War. And also, the feeling of fear continues because of the word "victims."

"The grandmother, Baby Suggs, was dead, and the sons, Howard and Buglar, had run away by the time they were thirteen years old—as soon as merely looking in a mirror shattered it (that was the signal for Buglar); as soon as two tiny hand prints appears in the cake (that was it for Howard)."

I'm picking up on ghostly behavior here. A shattered mirror and prints appearing in a cake sound like a spirit is walking among them.

"Neither boy waited to see more; another kettleful of chickpeas smoking in a heap on the floor; soda crackers crumbled and strewn in a line next to the door-sill. Nor did they wait for one of the relief periods: the weeks, months even, when nothing was disturbed. No. Each one fled at once—the moment the house committed what was for him the one insult not to be borne or witnessed a second time."

Here, I'm thinking about their emotions and how fear overcame them. The boys leave but Sethe, Denver, and Baby Suggs are left behind. I'm curious to know why they didn't feel compelled to leave. Was there a reason why they didn't leave? Hmmm... I need to keep reading to answer that question.

"What within two months, in the dead of winter, leaving their grandmother, Baby Suggs; Sethe, their mother; and their little sister, Denver, all by themselves in the gray and white house on Bluestone Road. It didn't have a number then, because Cincinnati didn't stretch that far. In fact, Ohio had been calling itself a state only seventy years when first one brother and then the next stuffed quilt packing into his hat, snatched up his shoes, and crept away from the lively spite the house felt for them.

I'm still wondering why Sethe and Denver didn't leave. Something kept them there, but after this first paragraph, I still do not know. Are these events connected to the women, but not the boys?

Supporting Students

When reading a complex text, students will need guidance and assistance. Allow them to read a text with a partner, using a think-aloud as they navigate the passage. Invite them to use the same strategy by stopping to ask questions and summarizing what they've read.

WE DO

Inviting Students to Be Vulnerable with Nonfiction

To help students navigate a nonfiction text, select a piece that you are unfamiliar with and complete a cold read of it in front of them, thinking aloud your strategy for unpacking the text. For me, an unfamiliar text would be one about Fortnite, the popular video game among today's teens. Placing an article such as "Apex Legends vs. Fortnite: The Battle for Battle Royal" by Tyler Anderson (2019) under the document camera, I read it aloud and make inferences about competition in the gaming world, such as how one game could be considered a threat, and why these games might be free and remain free for users. As I continue to read, I invite them to help me make sense of the text. My goal in this is to help them create schema for unpacking an unfamiliar text.

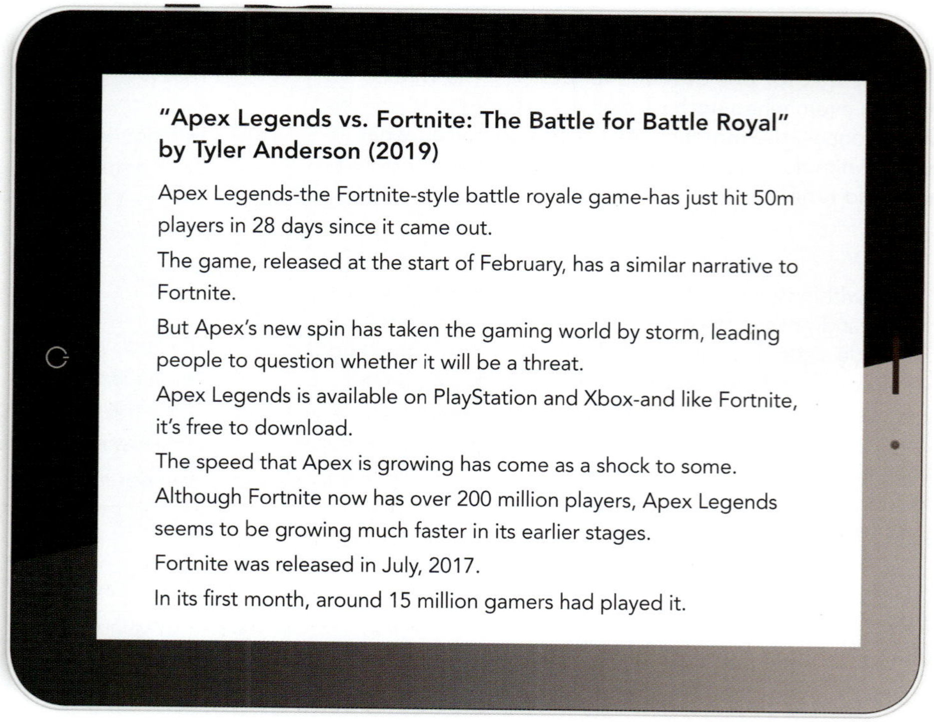

"Apex Legends vs. Fortnite: The Battle for Battle Royal" by Tyler Anderson (2019)

Apex Legends-the Fortnite-style battle royale game-has just hit 50m players in 28 days since it came out.

The game, released at the start of February, has a similar narrative to Fortnite.

But Apex's new spin has taken the gaming world by storm, leading people to question whether it will be a threat.

Apex Legends is available on PlayStation and Xbox-and like Fortnite, it's free to download.

The speed that Apex is growing has come as a shock to some.

Although Fortnite now has over 200 million players, Apex Legends seems to be growing much faster in its earlier stages.

Fortnite was released in July, 2017.

In its first month, around 15 million gamers had played it.

Supporting Students

When students encounter a complex text, they often feel a sense of defeat, assuming that this text, like all other difficult ones, is one that cannot be unpacked. They need help organizing strategies to assist them in understanding texts that may not be easily accessible to them. If several students appear lost, pull them together (or if a single student, join him or her), and go through part of the text with them. They may just need to see more of your process. Give them a chance to practice independently and check their understanding with a partner in the group (or with you, if it is a single student).

I would also suggest asking students to work with a partner to unpack complex texts often. A simple turn and talk gives students something to lean on as they work through challenging reading. Give them space and permission to struggle with this process.

Collegial Conversations

It was Tom Newkirk's *The Art of Slow Reading* (2012) that challenged my thinking about time and practice inside the classroom. Fluency is equated with speed, and is deliberate. Focused reading is abandoned in favor of timed reading passages, essays, and electronic forms of assessment—all in the name of data. A chaos of misconception exists about students' need for time to dive into texts and think beside them, and their learning needs are superseded by obsessive assessment, aimed at measuring accuracy and speed. We have to change this paradigm so students can recognize that their slower reading pace is a blessing, not a curse.

Management TIP

When demonstrating a think-aloud strategy for students, I not only show them my process, but I also try to think like them. I think about the questions they would have with a similar text and how my experience as a reader can encourage them to start noticing more. Specifically, your thinking aloud helps readers to:

- notice and question and unpack elements of a text, and how they are functioning
- realize that during reading readers do not always fully comprehend the text all the time—it's okay to read on even with unanswered questions as long as one understands enough
- Authors purposefully write texts in ways that "withhold" information and create moments of uncertainty for a reader, because that develops suspense, plot, and momentum.

Students take risks as readers when we take risks in modeling vulnerabilty.

YOU DO Honoring Vulnerability

Leaning in to students' thinking as they read and reflect is an important aspect of my role as a teacher guiding a Reader's Workshop. When students reflect on their reading experiences, think-alouds are elements that they say help them examine a text more closely. During check-ins, students mention how think-alouds give them a strong scaffold to think through complex and simple texts because they encourage them to notice.

When I recognize that a student is taking a risk with interpretation and reflective thinking, I will say, "Wow, I can tell you are thinking really hard about this book, and I really like the direction your ideas are going! Thank you for stretching your thinking." I love watching kids use my cold read think-aloud as a model to interpret texts, and when they do, I honor the hard work they're doing. I want them to persevere with a book, and to take risks with the interpretations they offer. This risk-taking is what leads to more sophisticated thinking about texts.

Supporting Students

Most students are not used to reflective thinking and, in their first attempts, they will wonder if they're even doing it right. If they're going to grow as readers and complex thinkers about texts, I need them to stick with it, to keep trying, and to evaluate their own abilities. Some students and even some adults assume that reading is passive, requiring nothing from the reader when, in fact, it is an active process, one that demands cognitive attention.

> Most students are not used to reflective thinking, and in their first attempts, they will wonder if they're even doing it right.

Reflections from Tanner's Notebook

Tanner's reading life lacked variety and volume at the beginning of the school year. He was hesitant to step outside his comfort zone as a reader, and tended to write or say clipped responses and reflections. He was also concerned about getting answers "right." I kept encouraging him, though, knowing that he needed to dwell beneath the surface. He began reading dystopian fiction later in the year, moving away from realistic fiction, and after reading *A Long Walk to Water* by Linda Sue Park (2010) and *Refugee* by Alan Gratz (2017), he realized that his reading identity was different than he had thought; finding these two novels gave him the confidence he needed in book selection and in articulating his responses to texts.

Like many students, Tanner grew more confident about his book selections due to choice and reflection.

Portrait Gallery of Student Growth

Tanner

Using Tweets to Unpack a Reading Life
Beginning-of-the-Year Reflection

Book: *Took* by Mary Downing Hahn

This book was good. It had good mystery elements.

My Take: Here, Tanner offers a brief review of the book—and nothing else. In my feedback, I asked him to dig deeper: What were those good mystery elements? What made them "good"? What draws you to mystery stories?

TRY THIS

Students at this juncture of loving a book or a genre are poised to take a leap forward with reflection, because the engagement is there. I'd ask questions that help students say why they enjoyed this book. When we talk about books we love, we refer to the book often, mentioning character change, scenes, plot, passages, and our unique take on them. Nudge students to reflect in ways that are persuasive.

End-of-the-Year Reflection

Book: ***Refugee*** **by Alan Gratz**

I fell in love with this book and I couldn't stop reading. After reading A Long Walk to Water, I wanted something else that would show me hardship and the truth of humanity. This book has taught me the delicacy of sanity and ever-looming threat of our only lifeline being taken away.

My Take: There is very noticeable shift in Tanner's thinking—he is now willing to reveal more of his thinking process, and also what he has learned. Refugee by Alan Gratz gave him a new perspective, and his thinking is now turned toward what the book has taught him. There is the sense, too, that Refugee has moved him one step closer to taking a stand that, in the future, a book might compel him to take action in some manner.

TRY THIS

Tanner is at a place in his reading life where he now knows what it's like to have a deep response to a book, one that makes you want to effect change in the world as a result of story. It is here, on this threshold, that I want him next to consider what the book taught him, and how the author brought about this call to action. When Tanner reads another book that moves him, he needs somewhere to go; I would ask him to think about what he might want to do, such as writing to the author, reading another book on a similar topic, sharing with classmates, or some other "outward" response.

Supporting Readers at Moments of Vulnerability

Checking in (or, conferring) with students is a great time to establish connections with them, as well as determine the skills they need more practice with. It's also a wonderful place to meet students where they are and honor the level of readiness with which they are approaching a text.

Olivia, a student in my class this year, explained on her interest inventory that she was not a reader and had never read and loved a single book. She loved listening to stories, but reading them and connecting had never happened. Tears flowed from her eyes as she shared her story, and something told me that, deep down inside, she wanted to know what falling in love with a book felt like.

> It's also a wonderful place to meet students where they are and honor the level of readiness with which they are approaching their blossoming reading lives.

In reading conferences, Olivia could regurgitate facts about a story, but describing how the book made her feel was a challenge. When I posed questions such as "What are you thinking about while you read this book?" or "How did the end of that book make you feel?", she would shrug her shoulders and just stare at me. Part of her struggle was understanding why she should care about imaginary people.

Supporting Olivia

I encouraged Olivia to read nonfiction, hoping to tap into her interest in sports and music, but she kindly declined. Because Olivia was at a fragile place in her reading life, I was careful not to injure any of her progress as a reader. I do not want to alienate any students. The creation of questions can be precarious if they are framed in a way that forecloses on any experience or reaction students may have. Although I wanted all students to take note of how their thinking about characters had changed, I knew Olivia would feel excluded because she was still trying to develop emotional thinking in regard to literature. To include her in this activity, I asked that my class respond to one of two questions:

- How has your thinking about the central character in your book changed since you started reading your book?
- What do you know about the central character now that you did not know when you started the book?

When I collected notebooks and scanned each one for the Tweet-length response, I noticed Olivia had chosen to respond to the second question instead of the first one. I was happy because that is one step closer to examining her own thinking about the books she reads.

Readers, like all of us, have various vulnerabilities. Meet them where they are, name their strengths, and remember Eve Merriam's wisdom: "It takes a lot of slow to grow."

Collegial Conversations

Often in education, we discuss the importance of perseverance in reading; in other words, how can we get students to become habitual readers and sustain that activity throughout their lives? A research study entitled *Teaching Adolescents to Become Learners: The Role of Noncognitive Factors in Shaping School Performance* stated that, "students are more likely to demonstrate perseverance in school if the school or classroom context helps them develop positive mindsets and effective learning strategies . . . teachers can lead students to exhibit greater perseverance and better academic behaviors in their classes through attention to academic mindsets and the development of students' metacognitive and self-regulatory skills…" (in *The Book in Question: How and Why Reading is in Crisis* by Carol Jago).

When Teaching Nonfiction

Teaching students to reflect about nonfiction is beneficial because it gives them an authentic reason to first understand what the author is saying—and then consider what they themselves think and feel about it. In this sense, reflection gives them more skin in the game; they realize that they are not merely engaged in the traditional school game of getting-facts-correct. But, make no mistake, analytical work with nonfiction is challenging. It begins with being clear on what makes reading fiction and nonfiction similar—and different. Educators Renee Houser and Gravity Goldberg in *What Do I Teach Readers Tomorrow?* (2017) invite us to approach the two kinds of reading via the kinds of thinking we tend to do. For fiction, for example, the operative work is around understanding character and interpreting theme. For nonfiction reading, it's synthesizing information and considering perspectives. By tightening the focus on these types of thinking, we can develop lessons, confer, and invite reflection with greater purpose and precision.

Kylene Beers and Robert Probst help crack open the strategies involved in considering perspectives with a series of questions well-pitched to root out an author's intentions:

- What are you thinking about while you read?
- What surprised you?
- What does the author believe?
- What language does the author use to make me feel a certain way?
- What does the author assume I know?
- What has challenged, confirmed, or changed your thinking?

(adapted from Beers & Probst)

Reading nonfiction requires students to keep track of their thinking while they read. Christopher Lehman and Kate Roberts (2018) recommend creating a class anchor chart with students, a strategy I use often. I front-load them with mini-lessons that give students lots of different choices for how to set goals for reading and how to track information. Following are just a few of the thinking moves I model and we record on anchor charts, and that permeate students' Reader's Notebook entries about nonfiction.

 |

When We Read and Take Notes with Nonfiction

- We underline and take notes to remember information, and also to ask questions and placehold our thinking.
- We think about the author and what the purpose of the text might be—to inform? To persuade? To Entertain? All three?
- What words signal that the author wants me to think in a particular way about this topic?
- We look for specific answers for what we are curious or confused about.
- We make connections by noticing headings, repeated words, and what the author seems to keep circling back to as an idea.
- We use two-column lists, circles, pictures, graphs—whatever we want—to help us visualize the material better and make connections and understand relationships.
- We reread to repair our confusion or to re-appreciate something that has struck us.
- We read illustrations and graphics, and know that understanding visuals may help us understand the words on that page.

When We Reflect About Nonfiction

- We reread our notes and may star or underline what stands out as something we understand really well or still need to clarify our thinking about.
- We think about the ideas we have about the topic as a result of this reading.
- We think about why we read this book in the first place, and whether the text changed our thinking, and how.
- We may reflect on specific challenges of the text, what we did to get through them, and if this book helped us reach a goal we had as readers.
- We use facts and quotes to help organize our reflection and give it power.
- We articulate how our thinking has changed over time.
- We look back at our notes to see if a visual we drew inspires a structure for our reflection or that we can develop as a picture with labels.
- We consider if we still have questions, or if this text made us curious about a subtopic or something new.
- We connect this work to another book, movie, or current event.
- We reflect on what we are moved to do as a result of this reading experience.

YOU DO Analytical Thinking with V.I.P. Words and Sentences

I use this strategy to push students back into the text to make an analytical decision. I think this activity works because it's so focused—students think about an author's use of language and vocabulary in a text.

What I say

I ask students to identify the most important sentence or the most important word in something they have just read. Most often, they use their independent reading books as a place to look for the most important words or sentences, but I have asked students to look at poems, songs, and even whole-class texts.

What students do

Once they make their decision, they write the chosen sentence or word inside their notebooks and, in a sentence or two, explain why they made the choice they did. Students make judgments about the things they read because they bring their experience to any text.

They develop internal criteria that let them know what the most important word or sentence in the book, poem, or song is. Like Rosenblatt, I want to honor what they bring to the text, their aesthetic or efferent response. There is no correct answer, only their opinion and their interpretation.

> They develop internal criteria that let them know what the most important word or sentence in the book, poem, or song is.

An example from Deja's notebook

The most important word in *Smile* by Raina Telgemeier is "teeth." This is the most important word because it is the reason Raina is insecure. She gets braces but ends up falling and knocking out her two front teeth. Her dentist puts a small cast in her mouth to help her mouth heal, but she continues to feel insecure because kids at school want to know what happened.

Supporting Students

Over the course of the year, students will have multiple "most importants" inside their notebooks, and during reading conferences or whole-class discussions, they can share what they notice about the most important parts of the books they read. Did they capture big ideas? Characterization? Themes? Conflict? Such an exploration gives them insight into their reading lives, and it shows them the types of fiction, poetry, and nonfiction they enjoy reading, what they notice most, and what they might need to look for in future reading.

When Teaching Nonfiction

This strategy works well with nonfiction, too. Modeling how to identify the most important words and/or sentences is a great way to help students unpack an informational text. Using the same process, ask students to determine what they notice after reading several informational pieces. This may be completed during a whole-class text or with a text that students read independently. As they read informational pieces (memoirs, articles, a friend's personal narrative, a biography, and so on), this is a tool they can use. They can think about:

- What is the most important word?
- What criteria did I use to nominate this as the most important word?
- Why does this sentence stand out? What do I notice after reading several nonfiction texts?
- What words/sentences are standing out to me?
- What does that let me know?

WE DO Notebook Spreads to Capture the Imagery of Language

In Chapter 2, I wrote about two-page spreads, and how, inspired by Penny Kittle, I began finding language and images within my independent reading to drop on the page. Since creating a spread for *The Poisonwood Bible*, I have worked to create spreads for *The Astonishing Color of After* by Emily Pan, and *Why They Can't Write: Killing the Five-Paragraph Essay and Other Necessities* by John Warner. After crafting these spreads, I always share them with students, knowing that this is a tool that many of them will enjoy.

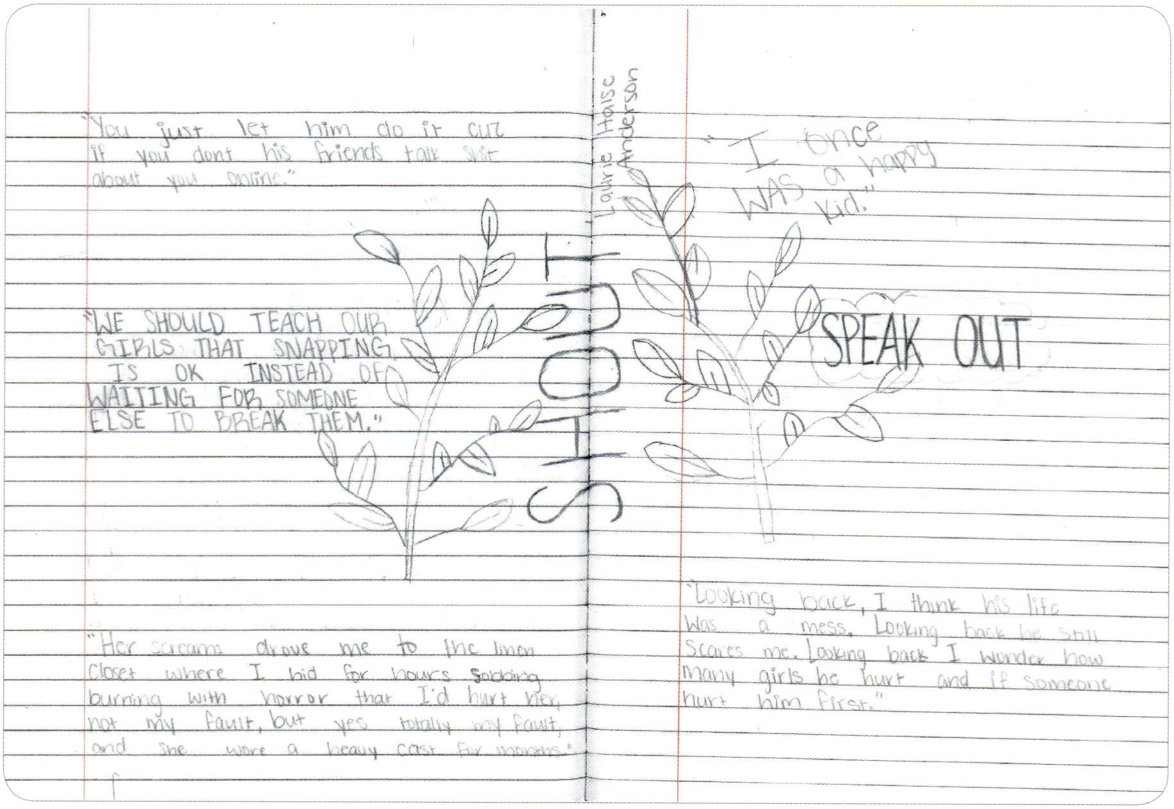

Mackenzie used *Shout* by Laurie Halse Anderson as inspiration for her two-page spread of beautiful language.

Supporting Students

Most often, I notice a little uncertainty because creating art in response to books is not something they are used to. In fact, many of them are still used to the tired read-question-answer format pervasive in ELA classrooms. Like other types of response and reflection, notebook spreads require students to notice and to evaluate. They decide, based on their reactions, what goes on the two-page spread. An example from a student is shown at left, and it speaks to the way creating these entries helps readers savor language. Reading and writing about reading cultivates creative thought, and seeds of ideas begin to sprout.

Once students finish a two-page spread, I ask them to "breathe in" their work and notice the things they captured, using these prompts:

- What types of sentences have I collected?
- Have I favored one narrator over another?
- What unites the ideas in these sentences?
- What do these sentences tell me about the novel?
- What do they tell me about myself and the types of things I notice when I read?

With these questions, students are uncovering their process. Their meditation on their work offers glimpses into their minds, once again making their thinking visible and applicable the next time they enter a story.

Management TIP

Penny Kittle (2019) suggests having students reflect after they complete multiple two-page spreads. Since beginning the journey with these spreads, I have adopted her idea, and I encourage students to reflect after they have created several in their notebooks. Depending on your group of kids, you may want to introduce this singular reflective process after one entry, or you may wish to wait until they have created several. Either way, I strongly recommend this type of response and reflection.

Responding and Reflecting on Nonfiction

Every so often, I share my professional reading with students because, ultimately, that reading influences their learning lives. After reflecting on *Why They Can't Write* by John Warner, I placed my notebook page under the document camera and gave students a moment to study it. Then I asked, "Can you tell I learned a lot from this book?" Together, we discussed several excerpts. When students see us as learners beside them, they recognize that a learning community exists, one where we are all growing and changing.

My two-page spread as a reflection for *Why They Can't Write* by John Warner.

Responding and Reflecting on Fiction

When I share my notebook pages devoted to Emily X.R. Pan's *The Astonishing Color of After*, I hope students would pick up on how moved I was by the evocative language of this novel, and how the author made me feel immersed in the Taiwanese culture. I invite students to share what they notice and, through our discussion, they gain a sense of how readers in a way learn about life along with the characters.

> "Can you tell I learned a lot from this book?" I asked them.

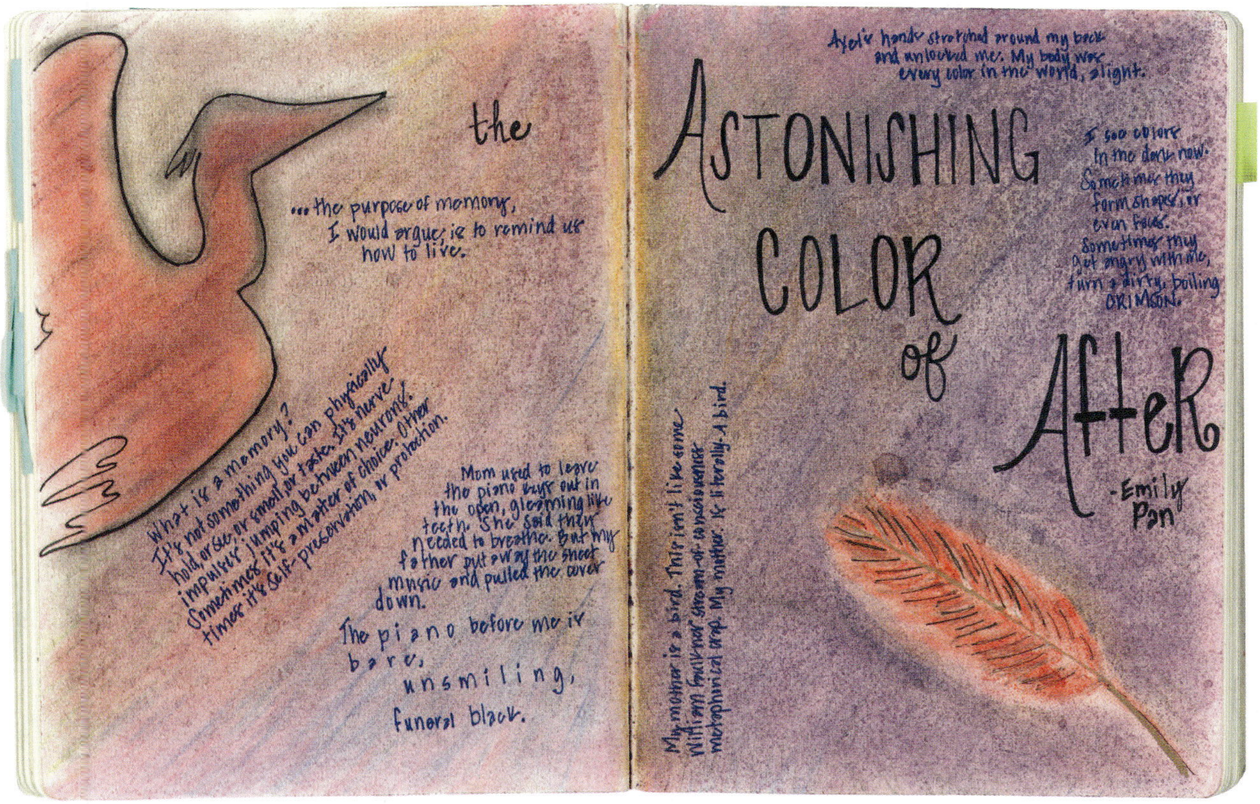

My two-page spread as a reflection for *The Astonishing Color of After* by Emily X. R. Pan.

Reflection Creates Changes in Thinking

In his notebook, Connor wrote:

> When I first started reading *Winger* by Andrew Smith, I thought Joey was just this character who chased after everyone and wouldn't have much to do with the story. At the end of the second book, *Stand-Off*, I realized that he was actually a very caring person and he wanted to help people. He genuinely loved people, especially Ryan. I think I judged him too quickly.

Connor's response shows a change in thinking. Meanings and interpretations are fluid, and they develop and evolve as readers continue to think about texts and the characters and events housed within them (*Reader-Response Theory in the English Classroom*, Probst, 1994). For thinking to evolve, it's important for students *to return* to their responses, and notice and note changes in their interpretation. Most striking about Connor's response is the admission that he judged Joey's character too quickly.

Meanings and interpretations are fluid, and they develop and evolve as readers continue to think about texts and the characters and events housed within them.

Supporting Connor

I would like to learn more from Connor about his experience of this book, especially since he recognized something within himself as a reader, and felt an emotional connection to the character. During a reading conference, I will ask Connor what he thinks this reveals about himself as a reader, and then ask him to write his ideas in his notebook. This might be a window into future interpretations of texts in his reading life, especially when he encounters characters similar to Joey in *Winger*.

Management TIP

A note about understanding the "Why". Often, in studying to become language arts teachers, we are trained to ask students to identify conflict and resolution, point out moments of character change, chart foils and foes, discuss a theme, and so on. Ah, but we neglect to explain to students why what we are asking is worthwhile. In the speed of teaching and assessing, we flatten these things for kids. As a result, our readers' reflections flatten too. By contrast, when we help students see the "Why" of the author's "What", for example noticing character turmoil and change is rather like a "superpower" of being a fiction reader, they take on that superpower! Connor was able to assert that *Winger* is about the teenage mind and how relationships influence and significantly change who we are and who we will become. In a nutshell, getting good at interpreting characters and their dynamics is like a secret backdoor to understanding an author's theme.

I DO Analyze Our Reflection with 3 Big Questions

Once reflections have landed in the reader's notebook, we have a better idea of where we are and where we need to go in our learning. I prefer that students have several reflective pieces, usually 5–10, generated inside their notebooks before we start to analyze them. The reflections are important when they stand alone; however, looking at several pieces of reflection as a group gives students and me a more incisive look into their minds.

I prefer that students have several reflective pieces, usually 5–10, generated inside their notebooks before we start to analyze them.

When students look at their own reflections, I ask them to determine:

1. what they notice about their reading lives, such as trends in their reading, genres they prefer, the number of pages they have read, and so on

2. what they notice about themselves as readers and thinkers (i.e. are they growing as a reader?), and

3. what they feel they need to do next as a result of these noticings.

I model this for students by putting my notebook under the document camera and sharing with them reflective pieces from my notebook. I place sticky notes on the pages I want to discuss with students, and after I share my reflections with them, I write my answers to these three questions. I do this as they are watching me, using a think-aloud strategy (Wilhelm, 2001).

Supporting Students

Kids will need a lot of support to analyze their reflections with these three questions, and I continue to model again and again how I look back at my reflections and allow them to guide my ideas. At first, this analysis is wobbly, and students may find it difficult to make sense of their reactions to their own thinking. I realize this because reflection challenges me. Looking across my own work takes time, and in some cases, courage—it is not always easy to look back to where you were. To assist students in this process, I collect notebooks every other week and read over the reflections. I write notes in the margins and highlight pieces that I feel show growth, either big or small.

During reading check-ins, I will point out these comments, and ask them to consider allowing my feedback to guide their thinking when we do analyze our reflections with the 3 Big Questions.
If they uncover something about themselves through our conversation, I ask them to jot down their ideas in their notebooks. This is especially important for striving readers.

Zachary is sharing his answers to 3 Big Questions with Antonio and Osmar. His willingness to share his answers gives them an idea of reflection they can do in their own notebooks.

Supporting Students

When I look at these reflections, I try to identify the places where students need further teaching and coaching. I look for places where students need help with:

- Understanding character
- Identifying the problem in a story (fiction or nonfiction), and analyzing the pathway to solving that problem
- Unpacking unfamiliar vocabulary
- Making connections across texts (intertextuality)
- Identifying and analyzing big ideas & themes
- Recognizing the craft moves an author uses to take a reader through a story
- Making judgments about characters, and tracking that thinking across a text

I want students to develop autonomy as readers, notice things in books, identify the craft an author uses to tell a story, generate their own valuable thinking, and pay attention to the ways their thinking changes over the course of a text.

> I collect notebooks every other week read and read over the reflections. I write notes in the margins and highlight pieces that I feel show growth, either big or small.

 |

Students need time to sit with a text and to let their minds roam, meander through thoughts about the ways people are represented, identify the issues they are grappling with, and explore the statement an author is making about life, and about people. I want students to do this work independently, but without chances to read, think, and write, they will not develop the automaticity they need to reach independence.

Bringing It All Together

Students may struggle with the reflective process, especially in the beginning stages. The thinking that students will do early in their reflections will more than likely be shallow, lacking the complexity and depth we want to see from them. Starting small with questions and gradually releasing the more difficult pieces of reflective thinking provides students with the necessary scaffold for metacognition. Using this structure helps students become more adept at looking back across their experiences and assessing their own learning.

When children realize through reading and reflection that they, in a sense, have a say in what the text means and why it's memorable, it's profound. It is a one-way trip to student agency, too.

I use story as a metaphor across the year when I discuss reflections with students. Thomas Newkirk's (2014) *Minds Made for Stories* posits the idea that our minds are constantly seeking a story—characters involved in a conflict who are seeking a resolution. It's how our brains work. I want students to see reflection as a story of their learning, and to see the challenges or problems they encounter, and decide how to solve those problems. Statements such as, "I think I did well," or "I really like this part of the book," are not necessarily bad reflections, but they do not give a window into the stories of learning. Strong questions, engaging activities, and time prompt deeper reflection and move students into critical thinking about their work as readers. A story emerges.

QUESTIONS to ASK YOURSELF

- **Craft a Tweet-length response and a series of hashtags related to the book you are currently reading. What do you notice about your process for creating these? How will this understanding help you in your classroom?**
- **Risk-taking and failure are avoided by students and teachers alike. How do you honor vulnerability in your classroom, and how can you encourage students to continue taking risks and possibly failing, even in a climate where both are frowned upon?**
- **Create a notebook spread of language and imagery to share with your students. What do you notice about what you've created? What challenges did you have to overcome to create your own spread? How will this impact your classroom?**

Concluding Thoughts: Embracing

In this chapter, the following ideas have been explored:

- Invitational language welcomes students into the reflective process.
- Twitter, hashtags, and freewrites give students a range of options to think about their reading.
- Reflection tells the story of students' learning—it can be used as an assessment tool for them and for you in determining what they need and where they need to go.

From this point, after you have determined that students are prepared for more rigorous forms of reflection, it is time to start considering how they can own the process. Owning the reflection process requires automaticity in the sense that students are able to reflect independently of the instructor. Assessing where students are in the process means identifying how students are thinking and responding. I usually use the four aptitudes I introduce below to determine if students are ready to move into deeper waters of reflection. Students who are demonstrating an understanding of how reflection works are prepared to more rigorously analyze the story of their learning.

The Four Aptitudes

1. **Being intentional** by using reflective tools with purpose
2. **Identifying when reflection is necessary**
3. **Making connections** between their reflections and their growth and progress as readers, and
4. **Applying** their knowledge to their reading lives as well as the world around them.

Collegial Conversations

Metacognition, or thoughts about thoughts (i.e. reflection), is where the real power of learning resides. When we think about our thoughts, hypothesizing about the "Why "behind the ideas we generate, we find clarity in our process and can move forward based on what is revealed. Hartman (1998) notes that metacognition includes acquisition, retention, and application of what is learned, as well as critical thinking and problem-solving. This host of skills, from acquisition to evaluation, is housed within the context of reflective thinking. Eventually, after multiple chances to think reflectively and consider where we are as readers, thinkers, and learners, metacognition becomes reflexive—we read, pause, reflect, and react, moving along a spectrum of thinking.

CHAPTER 6

Owning Reflection for a Lifetime

In this final chapter, I try to catch one, last, wild thing with my bare hands: the reflector and reader in the wild (Miller, 2013). Like sighting the rare Red Lorikeet in a rainforest, I notice and track students' independence with a lot of patience, observation, and reverence. To know the signs that your students are ready to be more independent with reflection, let's begin with a fuller look at the four aptitudes—think of them as behaviors to watch for in students' actions, conversations, and writing.

"Like sighting the rare Red Lorikeet in a rainforest, I notice and track students' independence with a lot of patience, observation, and reverence.

S. Travis Crowder"

Habits that Show the Four Aptitudes

As I introduced in Chapter 4, the majority of students should demonstrate an essential understanding of being intentional, identifying when reflection is necessary, making connections, and applying their knowledge. I refer to these strengths as the Four Aptitudes. Here are some student habits to watch for:

1. Students are **being intentional** when they are able to choose a reflective tool and name why they are choosing it for a reflection.
2. Students are **identifying when reflection is necessary** when they listen to their hearts as they read and are noticing intersections in their reading where stopping to write and notice are important.
3. Students are **making connections** when they understand how reflections assist their growth and progress as readers and how reflection can help them better understand and influence their world.
4. Students are **applying their knowledge** when they use reflection to push themselves further as readers and thinkers and use it to effect change in their world.

We observe and celebrate students' growth with the same attention and reverence we have for rare beauty in the wild.

Routines for Formative Assessment

When do we quicken the pace and start pushing for student readers to take on more of the "You Do"? There is no magic time, but it often begins after the first grading period. Some years, you may want to wait until after the first semester. Just keep in mind that reflections belong to students, and where they are as reflective readers will determine their readiness to move forward. They are the driver; you are the passenger. And it begins with both you and students getting a handle on where they are as reflective readers.

> Students are applying their knowledge when they use reflection to push themselves further as readers and thinkers and use it to effect change in their world.

Students Self-Assess

Invite students to use previous reflections as mentor texts for writing a reflection about the journey so far. At first, students will feel uncertain, believing that reliance on scaffolding (e.g. providing written instructions) is critical. Still, I encourage them to use previous reflections as a mentor text for newer ones. It helps students assess themselves because they can write a reflection without prompting.

Read Student Reflections

When I read through their reflections, and consider what I have learned about them in check-ins and group discussions, I can determine when students are prepared to handle the heavier moves of reflection. Their writing informs the decisions I make as a teacher — do I need to meet with them one-on-one, or is there a more pervasive issue, one that requires a mini-lesson?

Plan Future Instruction & Conferring

Using a status-of-the-class checklist, determine which students you want to pull into a small group to give support. Which students are the high flyers who might support their peers? What mini-lessons might provide models of being an independent reader? Use the If/Then chart on the facing page as a springboard for other "Ifs" to look for and possible instructional supports. I admire Laura Robb and Evan Robb's notion of both listening and looking for as we formatively assess, so I now like to call any If/Thens I consider Listen and Look Fors.

Listen and look for students who are ready to support others with reflection.

Listen & Look Fors

If	Then
Students are reading . . .	They are prepared to respond to questions and ideas in their notebooks. (See Questions that Elicit Responses, page 13.)
Students are having difficulty finding books they are interested in reading . . .	They need to articulate the reasons why books are not meeting their needs (with teacher help) and return to their interest inventory to consider the topics and subjects that are of interest to them. They may also need to consult a friend, review the books that have been discussed in class, or return to a favorite from years past.
Students are engaging with their books and writing solid responses . . .	They are prepared to start thinking reflectively about their reading and their reading lives, using the tools for reflection (i.e. hashtags, Tweets, and freewrites).
Students are struggling to write responses and to feel . . .	They need teacher feedback, explicit instruction, discussion with a partner, and/or questions to help them unpack their responses to their reading. They may also need help with developing the language to express their feelings. Further direct instruction, the creation of a class anchor chart, and checking-in with students to help them make sense of their emotions and reactions are a few ways to cultivate students' connections to books
Students are struggling to understand how to use a particular tool . . .	They may need more practice, more explicit instruction, and/or help from a partner. A self-stick note listing tools inside their reading notebooks may be helpful in reminding them
A student or several students are finding it difficult to choose their own tool to reflect . . .	You might try helping them narrow the parameters by encouraging them to think about characters' changes or a most important word.
Students are having a difficult time writing their reflections . . .	They may need to talk it out with a partner or with you. They may also need you to transcribe for them until they get the hang of it.
Students are noticing how tools can be used intentionally (such as using a Tweet to help them narrow their focus, using a freewrite to get all their thoughts on paper, or using hashtags to capture big ideas) . . .	They are prepared to begin selecting their own tools to use independently.
Students show a consistent preference for a particular tool . . .	Allow them to honor that preference, but encourage them to try something different.
Small groups of students or even one student shows an ability to notice nuances between response and reflection and demonstrates an aptitude for reflection earlier than other students . . .	Allow that student/those students to choose their tool of preference when they need to.

Lessons That Invite the World

Students engaged in books of their choice and reading steadily throughout the year — that's pretty darn good, right? With smart phones and the digital universe tugging at everyone's attention, can we expect more? Yes, we can. We want to keep providing ideas that actually motivate kids to read. We do this by talking up various genres. We do this by being as "real" with students about how much say that have as readers about when, what, and how they read. The following are some favorite teaching ideas.

Drop It: When to Abandon a Book

Imagine looking over on an airplane and seeing a person in his mid-forties reading a book all the way from New York to California, looking bored out of his mind. You ask him what's going on, and he says, "I can't stand this book but I have to finish it." Of course, that would never happen. Worldly readers give up on books all the time, and so we have to reinforce that reality to students. I'll tell my students that if I begin reading a book that does not capture my attention after three or so chapters, I will put it aside and find something more interesting.

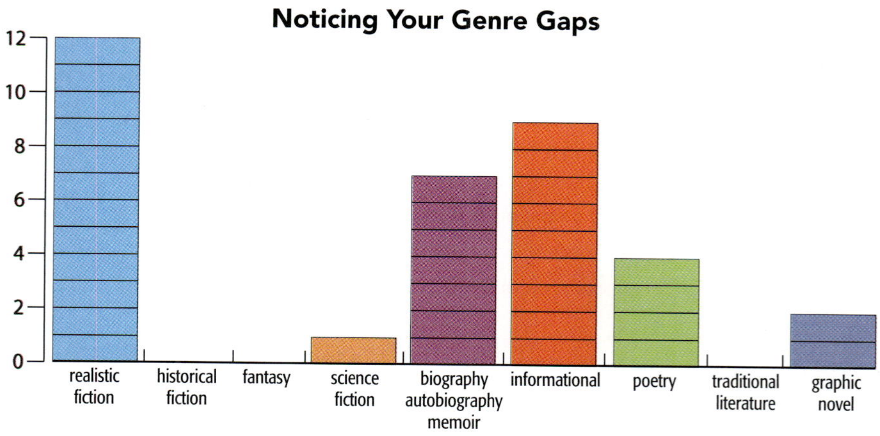

Complete your own genre gap inventory and share with students. Let them see the genres you have avoided and reflect in front of them. Set goals so they see you participate in the process. This graph idea was adapted from *Reading in the Wild* (2013) by Donalyn Miller with Susan Kelley.

Supporting Students

When students abandon a book, I ask them during a check-in: Why did you choose to stop reading this book? Most often, I hear "because it was boring," and they turn away to find another read. I press them further, though: What specifically about the book did you find boring? The characters? The pace of the novel (i.e. was it not moving quickly enough)? The subject matter? When students answer these questions it can help them form their reading identity as well as help them select future books.

When students view writing about reading as valuable in their lives, they do it happily, on their own time. Even as a solo activity, it has a social dimension because the reader often communes with the characters, and thinks about sharing her reflection with others.

Scratching an Itch: Writing Out of Urgency

Ideally, readers should write when they need to, when it's what Peter Elbow (1998) calls "the itch" to write. For example, perhaps a student has read Billy Collin's poem "Litany" and it inspired him to write his own version of it. Maybe a news story moves your students to action and you want them to capture that thinking in their notebooks. Or, a child has just read a tragic part in his independent reading book, and the strong emotional connection causes him to cry, mourning for the loss a beloved character.

Supporting Students

These moments merit reflection. We support students by looking and listening for them, and daring to suggest verbal or written reflection on the spot. I encourage you to consider how reflection can be a system of thinking inside your classroom, not just a once-a-week assignment ...let it grow from a place of curiosity and love.

Consider how reflection can be a system of thinking inside your classroom.

Be the Change: Write to Influence the World

During faculty meetings, I often hear the statement that we are preparing students for the real world, as though the real world was a place students go only after they have graduated. We do not do the hard work of literacy for children to affect the world later; instead, we want them to read, write, and think in ways that will affect their world now. Students need to see the function of literacy in their lives, its function beyond the walls of a classroom. When we isolate reading and writing about reading as classroom assignments, we drain the power of literacy and make it about compliance. Instead, I want literacy to be about defiance. After all, all valuable inventions, works of art, and scientific breakthroughs come from someone seeing something anew, and acting. Think back to Brittani's reflection in Chapter 1, (pp. 24-25). It shows the stirrings of an individual beginning to let down her guard and allow books to trigger bigger questions about society.

Invite students to generate a list of things they can do to influence their world. These actions may include letters to the editor, the school board, or videos to raise awareness.

Dare to Share: Activities for Revealing Voice

Most kids will want to share the things they uncover in their books, and like most communities that are based around reading, conversation about characters and discoveries within a text will flood small and large groups of students. When students go from text to answering readymade comprehension questions to more texts and more questions, there is no authenticity to the work; instead, the busywork of fake readers sets in, where students adopt the habits associated with compliant reading and boredom. The work of a reflective reader includes opportunities to hold thinking inside our minds and hearts, hold it inside our notebooks, and chances to share that thinking with a peer, teacher, or group of people. To help students share their reflections, consider the following opportunities:

> The work of a reflective reader includes opportunities to hold thinking inside our minds and hearts.

Activity: Gaps in Our Reading Diets

(Miller & Kelley, 2013)

- Distribute copies of Noticing Your Genre Gaps bar graph.
- Explain that our reading preferences inform the shape of our reading lives. Part of being a well-rounded reader is venturing into reading territory outside of our comfort zones.
- Project a copy of your reading gap bar graph. Let them tell you what they notice, such as the genres you prefer and the genres you have avoided.
- Give them time to work on their own, cut it out, and paste it inside their notebooks. I usually ask students to put theirs on the inside back cover.
- Ask: What genres have you avoided? Why do you feel you have avoided them?

To extend this activity, I place stacks of books around the room that correlate with each genre on the bar graph. Students can go to each table and spend time browsing different titles. I ask them to add titles they feel they might enjoy to their "to-read" lists. Once they are finished perusing the different genres, I give them time to chat with a partner or write in their notebooks about their experiences with the reading diet gap activity. They can write or talk about a book they found that they think they would enjoy, what they've learned about themselves as readers, or a goal they would like to set to push themselves out of their comfort zones.

Collegial Conversations

As students develop a habit of reflective thinking, their ideas expand from introspection to deeper levels, where we need them to go if they are to "own" the process of reflection. John Powers' (Gallagher, 2004, p. 157) work with *Circles of Reflection* show self at the center. As one looks outward, reflection begins to include family, peers, community, country, and humankind.

Activity: A Text That Affected Me

Helping students name the books and ways that texts influence them is important for their growth and evolution as reflective thinkers. It is a critical lens through which they can view their reading. I introduce this to students by telling them a story about how a book has affected me. When I am affected by a text, my heart is pricked and I can't stop thinking about it. Then, I ask them to think about how books have affected them. What do they feel when a book really gets to them? I do ask them to participate by choosing a text that has affected them and writing about it inside their notebooks. By initiating this conversation with them, I want them to begin noticing and naming how books affect them.

Questions for Students

To help students identify and think about the books that have affected them, ask:

- What is a book that has touched your heart this year? Was it the characters, language, or circumstances in the novel that touched your heart the most?
- What did you feel when you read this book?
- At what point in the book did you start to feel this emotion? Will you find this passage and read it aloud to me?
- What have you noticed about yourself since you've read this book?

Agents of Change

The distance between a strong reading identity and a strong identity in the world is a mere hop, skip, and a jump. As I hope has been evident in the student samples throughout this book, the children we teach are at the beginning of their life journey. We see in their words glimmers of sustained, sophisticated thinking and sure-footedness. A child may be a realistic fiction devotee now, but switch to be a history buff after college. Students may read only newspapers as adults, or do most of their "reading" via listening to the radio. None of that matters. What matters is that they know their voice and their freedoms through the books they read now, as Lester Laminack and Katie Kelly said so well:

> *When the reader stands in his own world view, unable to see or conceive of any other perspective, a book can be a bridge. The right book, at the right time, can span the divide between where the reader stands in this moment and alternate views, new ideas, and other options not yet considered. Books as bridges enable the reader to speak freely, think deeply, and take action as a change agent (Laminack & Kelly, 2019).*

As students read the world through self-selected books and work associated with research, as well as texts that we share, such as poems, articles, read-alouds, and short stories, I want them to begin finding their unique voices as human beings. In this next set of lesson ideas, I emphasize this concept of a book as a call to action.

Becoming an Agent of Change

Recently, I read *White Rage* by Carol Anderson (2016), and the haunting history that she shares of racial disparity affected the conversations I am willing to have with my students. I felt an urgency because of Dr. Anderson's book, and aside from sharing it on social media and talking about it with friends, the important piece was how it influenced me and what I was willing to do because of that influence. Fiction has this power, too. *Beloved* by Toni Morrison was one of those books that created a sense of change within me, causing me to think about moral and ethical obligations differently. Discussing rightness and wrongness with students became more nuanced and conversation-based as opposed to identifying ethics and morality on our perceptions and biases. Kids need to hear how I respond and reflect about my reading, as well as how it moves me to act.

Discussing how literature affects us, plants seeds in students' hearts and minds. We plant them hoping they grow into mighty things.

I DO Influence the World

Writing for me is like ascending a spiral staircase, circuitous rather than linear, and even when I seem to stall, or stumble upon a surprising thought or connection, I always feel my thinking is elevated by writing to reflect. I am also in awe of how reflection may encourage me to influence my world. In other words, it's not entirely an inward looking act, but may have a social dimension. This is the dynamic I want to model for students periodically.

What I might say: "Have you ever read something and it just makes you want to do something? It's important for you to notice that reaction — that is your heart speaking to you. When I feel moved to action by a book, I go to my notebook and just write about it. Often, that writing leads me to what I need to do."

For example, reading about racial disparity and social injustice in Nic Stone's *Dear Martin* may nudge me to write about police brutality. Dashka Slater's *The 57 Bus* may influence me to write an opinion piece about identity. In both cases, I am thinking reflectively and working to influence their world — and my own.

> When I'm moved to action by a book, I go to my notebook and just write about it.

WE DO A Call to Action

To engage students in considering the books that have moved them emotionally, you may want to think about asking one or several of the following questions:

- Now that you've read this, what do you feel you should do?
- What is something you've read that you feel is compelling you to do something, such as write a letter, raise awareness for something, reach out to a friend, etc.?
- How does fiction compel us? How does nonfiction compel us?
- What nonfiction pieces (articles, videos, etc.) cause us to act?

Sometimes students just need to read more to deepen their understanding of a topic.

Supporting Students

Give kids time to consider books and/or pieces of writing that have influenced them to interact with their world. Most of the time, students have an idea thumping in their hearts and they feel drawn to write or to speak out about an issue or topic through a chosen medium. For students who need a little help mining their thinking, I sit beside them and ask them to go through their Reader's Notebooks with me. We look at reading we have done independently, as well as texts we have read together as a class. Questions initiate reflection and invite students into the process.

- Let's start with your "read" list. Is there a book here that you feel has moved you in some way?
- Is there a text that has made you question the world we live in?
- Is there a text with a social issue that you feel deeply connected to?
- Is there a text that has made you angry?
- Is there a text that has made you feel as though they need to speak out about something?
- Is there a character or person in a text whom you have connected with? If so, what happened, how did it happen, and how do you feel about it?

WE DO Taking a Stand Against Child Labor

Children are sensitive to social injustice — both current and historical. Discussing the history of child labor helps students get a sense for what "a call to action" feels like. I open with, "Today we are going to look at visual texts — photographs and a video. Visual texts still require reading but in a different way. They require us to listen and pay attention to the images. What I want you to do is pay attention to your reactions and what specific elements might be causing those reactions."

Lewis Hine, a well-known sociologist and photographer, used his skills at the turn of the 20th Century to expose the harsh reality of child labor. When I share these images with students, they are horrified that such conditions existed, but they are more horrified when I share that these conditions still exist around the world. I share images from Hine's book, as well as the video, "ABCs of Child Labor" from stopchildlabor.org. I ask them to notice what they were feeling and/or experiencing as they looked at and watched these texts. What do you feel and what words and specific images are causing you to feel that way? What can we do to help? Together we generate a list of things we could do which included:

> Visual texts still require reading, but in a different way. They require us to listen and pay attention to the images.

- Writing to the local paper to raise awareness about modern-day child labor
- Creating a Twitter or Instagram page to share information
- Writing letters to local, state, and federal government leaders to share our child labor concerns and ask what they are doing to combat the issue

Supporting Students

I ask students to write this list in their notebooks and as we continue to read and to react to texts, we update the list. Also, if we encounter a specific type of text, such as a poem, commentary, book review or video, that we feel would engage an audience and help influence the world, we add that to our class anchor chart and to our reading notebooks.

Images are complex texts. They invite analysis, reflection, and action.

Helping Students Handle Strong Reactions

Donald M. Murray once said that problems make good subjects (Atwell, p. 587). As students read powerful books across a year, they will start gravitating to certain topics, ones that may be considered controversial or sensitive. Topics may include abuse, addiction, racism, and bias. Young readers have a strong sense of justice; they want to see the truth or what is just and fair, prevail in the end. This next lesson channels their reactions toward action.

> Young readers have a strong sense of justice; they want to see the truth or what is just and fair prevail in the end.

I DO Notice and Name

To create an authentic atmosphere, and borrowing language from Peter Johnston's (2004) amazing book, *Choice Words*, I start with a mini-lesson where I begin with noticing and naming our reactions to our reading and helping students generate ideas of things they can do to effect change in their world. We may work on these ideas in our notebook or on a computer, but ultimately, I want students to do this work without prompting. Here are some strategies that have proved helpful in my classroom:

You want students to consider *how* the author instigated that feelng in a particular moment or the entire text.

- Help students name a reaction. You may give them frames to think about their reactions such as "This book makes me feel ______ because ______ ." . . or "When I read the part about ______ I had questions about __________. . ." Encourage readers to find the ideas that are resonating within their hearts.
- Move students into reflective thinking with questions. You may at first ask "What did you feel when you read this book?" but move into reflective territory by asking students to consider *how* the book or text created that feeling within them.
- Give personal examples. Share from your reading life the books that have moved and changed you. Put your notebook under a document camera or photocopy sections from books and/or your notebook for students to see. Bring them to life by explaining what you were feeling and how you turned those feelings into actions.
- Honor times when books lead us to silent or personal contemplation.
- Honor moments when students just need to write about their reading.
- Look back at poems from whole-class discussions. What words and phrases or images really grabbed your attention. How did the poet do that?

Students are ready to engage with serious and joyous topics of the world.

YOU DO When Students are Moved to Action

I begin the lesson by saying something like, "When you read, it is so important for you to listen to your heart. Your heart might be telling you it is time to act, and that is your cue to go inside your notebook and write what you're feeling and thinking about. This work will be independent, but when something calls to you, that's your cue to listen. What might you need to do? For example, if you've read a powerful book, such as *The Hate U Give*, by Angie Thomas (2017), what is a natural way for you to share your experience with that book?

Supporting Students

During check-ins, I pay attention to when a student is loving a book to the point of wanting to connect or "act" in some way. I will ask them if they have any thoughts on what they might want to say or share. Some students, however, need concrete avenues for responding. Here are a few ideas that scaffold students — but they aren't meant to be assigned. Students need to choose them when they wish.

- Write how this book has changed them
- Write a letter to a friend, family member, teacher, or leader
- Write a letter to the editor or a commentary
- Write to the author
- Share the book and their experience on Twitter, Instagram, or Facebook
- Create a video calling others to action
- Add a self-stick note recommendation inside the book
- Find movements or causes associated with the book and get involved with those

Let students decide what they need to do. They are the readers and they are the future. Releasing independence to them will make the end result powerful because it belongs to them.

WE DO Big Ideas

I introduce students to the concept of big ideas early in the school year. Big ideas have a beautiful utility because they invite everyone—thriving and striving readers—to the proverbial table. All students can work with big ideas because all students have experience with them. I've never met a student whose life did not include experiences with betrayal, struggle, hurt, pain, endurance, friendship, death, or loyalty. This emotional connection (transactive) with big ideas engages kids in analytical thinking (interpretive), a part of reflection that I want to nudge them toward.

To help students think and write about big ideas, consider the following points from my classroom:

- Keep an anchor chart of big ideas in the classroom
- Use short texts such as poems, informational pieces, or even an excerpt (if possible) to teach and/or to extend students' thinking about big ideas (Robb)
- Invite students to respond once every other week about a big idea they notice in their independent reading. Encourage them to include an example or two that supports the big idea
- Invite students to connect their books to a big idea in a text you have studied together, such as a poem, informational piece, or an excerpt

> All students can work with big ideas because all students have experience with them.

Variations to Try

Like all procedures, practice leads to application. And with continued practice, kids begin to internalize the process. You may want to try:

- Big idea notebooks (Kittle)
- Sticky notes
- The four most common big ideas in my reading life
- Grouping books based on big idea (whole-class activity)
- Book clubs

On the days we reflect on our reading lives, students are given the choice to write about big ideas, a piece of owning this process. I encourage them to notice patterns in their reading lives. What big ideas are you drawn to? What big ideas would you like to explore? As students continue to think beside their reading lives, patterns emerge, and I teach students to notice those patterns, using them to inform and to analyze their reading lives in reflection.

Students thrive when we sit beside them and discuss texts as fellow readers.

Full Circle: Reflection about Reflection

At this chapter's outset, I talked about asking students to reflect on their reflections near the end of the first semester. Circle back to this activity mid-year and toward the end of the year, so students notice how they've changed and how their reading lives have evolved.

Some changes will seem small, while others will appear dramatic. Keep in mind, though, that all changes are significant. Kids are human beings, and like all people, some will notice larger spans of growth than others, but that doesn't mean more means better. A small amount of change in students' reflections may show that they finally uncovered their reading identity. From a reflection later in the year, you may hear the whispers of book love, where a student might realize she doesn't despise reading as much as she thought she did.

A caution: it can sometimes be dismaying when toward the end of the year, there is a student who didn't seem to go as "far" as you thought he or she might, for whatever reason. Have faith — even though it may seem like a small change to you, it may feel like a monumental change for the child, as though he has finally "arrived." As mentioned earlier in the book, I ask students to look back at their reading reflections at several points in the year. You may find it helpful to ask them to take an assessment of their reading reflections at the end of the first semester and at the end of the second semester.

Portrait Gallery of Student Growth

Faith

Several years ago, Faith, a student whose prior experiences in language arts had left her with labels ("slow reader" and so on), fell in love with reading and writing and destroyed the myths that had been created about her. I watched her thinking grow and her notebook swell with response and reflection. Toward the end of the school year, we read "You Can't Write a Poem about McDonald's" (Atwell), and after some responses in our notebooks and class discussion, we wrapped up class, laughed about some of the descriptions in the poem, and once the afternoon announcements ended and the bell rang, students left for the day. The next morning, as I was writing the day's agenda on the board, Faith's voice broke my thoughts:

End-of-the-Year Reflection

"Mr. C," she began, "I was thinking about that poem yesterday. You know, the one about McDonald's. Well, it's strange because he said you can't write a poem about McDonald's, but he wrote a poem about it. I thought about that yesterday!"

My Take: *This epiphany is a shining example of reflection. The day before, Faith's response had been about meaning, metaphor, and imagery. But on her own, it hit her, the irony of Wallace's writing. When we read, we draw upon comprehension and feeling, and these two sources feed into each other, like two babbling brooks in the woods. Comprehension allows us to feel, and feeling increases our comprehension. There is a place, though, when we actually "get it," and we know the writing more intimately.*

TRY THIS

In a moment such as this, I want students to determine how their thinking came to be. I might ask, "What caused you to recognize this in the text?" or "How can this help you interpret other texts you encounter?" These questions encourage students to reflect on their growing understanding and transfer their new thinking to future texts.

 |

A Year of Reading Reflections

It's May and we are wrapping up a year of Reader's Workshop, highlighting the various reading reflections in our notebooks and typing ones that show growth in our reading lives. As they reflect about their reflections, they remember books they read earlier in the year — a time when most of them hated to read. That has changed significantly.

I hand out copies of the Year of Reading Reflections. I challenge them to identify a reflection that showed their abilities earlier in the year and another that showed them at their best. After identifying these two pieces, they typed them into a shared document on Google Classroom and spent time reflecting about the changes they noticed. Several students struggled to dig into these reflections and determine how they had changed as readers, but in their responses, they're noticing changes in themselves. I am, too.

I challenge them to identify a reflection that showed their abilities earlier in the year and another that showed them at their best.

Students' responses are very informative, and they help me assess their growth. I would argue that this type of assessment is the purest form we can offer, and superior to assigning a grade. It gives teacher and students meaningful, actionable insights. Standardized measures may tell where our students are in relation to everyone else and to the "standard" (an arbitrary term that is more nebulous than anything), but they will never tell the complete story of our students. Those stories reside inside of them, and the growth that they experience as readers and thinkers cannot be measured by a multiple-choice test. They are better understood when we consult students, the ones who are reading and thinking about texts.

Feel free to adapt the Year of Reading Reflections for your classroom.

Students need to own their learning, and we, the teachers, need to listen to that story.

A Year of Reading Reflections

Name ________________________________ Date ____________

Across this entire year, you have reflected each Friday to assess your progress as a reader and a thinker. This document is your opportunity to look back through the reflections and identify how you've grown. Feel free to name the tools that have been most beneficial to you, and what they have helped you learn about yourself.

Find an example of a Tweet that you practiced with earlier this year. Try to find one that you would consider your favorite. Add it to the box at right.	
Find an example of a Hashtag that you wrote earlier this year. Try to find one you consider your favorite. Add it to the box at right.	
Find an example of a reading reflection that shows where you were as a reader at the beginning of the year. It may be from the first week of school or several months into the school year. Add it to the box at right.	
Find an example of a reading reflection that shows you at your best this year. The example should display deep thinking and quality of analysis. Add it to the box at right.	
Look back across your reflections from this year, going one by one through them. Think about your ideas and your writing from the start of the year until now. When you have looked at all of them, answer the questions shown below: • Looking at your reflections, how do you feel you have grown as a reader this year? • Which tool has been most helpful to you as a reader? (Tweets, hashtags, freewrites, etc.) • What have you noticed about yourself as a reader as a result of using this tool? Ideas to consider including in your responses: How has your reading pace improved? How is it different now than it was earlier this year? What did your reflections help you to uncover about yourself? What genres did you find yourself writing about most often? How did writing about your reading help you as a reader? What did you notice you were accomplishing each week? What experiences did you have as a reader (such as wonder, fear, uncertainty, excitement)? Did your reflections help you think differently about your reading? If so, how? If not, what did you focus on in your writing?	
Have you noticed growth as a reader and thinker this year? How has your thinking about books/text changed? Write as much as you can to answer this question. When did you start noticing these changes in yourself? If you do not think you have changed, what challenges do you feel stood in your way? In what ways could you have pushed yourself as a reader/thinker? Write as much as you can to answer this question.	

Concluding Thoughts: Looking Back, Facing Forward

In this chapter, the following points have been explored:

- Students are prepared for independent reflection when they demonstrate an ability to be intentional with reflective tools, identify when reflection is necessary, make connections between the tools and their reading lives and selves, and apply their knowledge to their future reading as well as to the world around them.
- An understanding of self nurtures students' sense of the world around them and the ways they can affect positive change.
- Looking back at reflections across the year helps students understand how they've grown.

When students read with conviction and passion, they have the skill and the courage to move the world forward — one book at a time.

There is not a readymade formula for the work of real readers. No single strategy will help every reader because reading is such a personal, intimate act. To disrupt a student's process, in favor of a lesson plan, is to ignore the beautiful strands of thinking that have started to flow inside the heart and mind of that student. The best formula I can give, which isn't a formula at all, is for kids to constantly reflect on their reading, looking back at characters and people — at humanity — and deciding what their hearts are telling them to do. Sure, they'll need some help, and they'll need you to work alongside them. Eventually, they'll find their voices, their passions, and their reasons to take action.

As new students walk into my classroom each year and claim their seats, I know the task that awaits me. There will be kids whose eyes light up at the prospect of free-choice independent reading, and they'll be aching to inhale a new book as if it were oxygen. I'll also hear some groaning or see stares of disbelief when students hear that their year will be filled with reading, but I will promise them that I will move heaven and earth to help them find the right books, the ones that will speak to their interests.

Our world is desperate for literate human beings, ones who know the power of books, understand the need for reflection, and can use both to give the world hope. But more than anything, I know that reading and reflective thinking can help students grow into confident, intrepid readers who have the capacity to build a better version of themselves, and ultimately, a better version of the world.

QUESTIONS *to* ASK YOURSELF

- **What is a book that has stirred you to affect change in the world? How would this story affect your students?**
- **How has your writing changed since responding to the questions in the first chapter of this book? Has your writing deepened? Become more succinct? Become more authentic? How will this influence your teaching?**
- **What current events stir your emotions and call you to action? How can you bring these into the classroom and invite students to think about them alongside you?**

References

American Indians in Children's Literature. (n.d.) Retrieved from https://americanindiansinchildrensliterature.blogspot.com

Anderson, C. (2017). *White Rage. The Unspoken Truth of Our Racial Divide.* New York, NY: Bloomsbury.

Anderson, T. (2019). apex legends vs. Fortnite: The Battle for Battle Royal. BBC news.com

Atwell, N. (2014). *In the Middle: A Lifetime of Learning About Writing, Reading, and Adolescents* (3rd Ed.). Portsmouth, NH: Heinemann.

—. (2016). *Naming the World: A Year of Poems and Lessons.* Portsmouth, NH: Heinemann.

Atwell, N. & Atwell Merkel, A. (2016). *The Reading Zone: How to Help Kids Become Skilled, Passionate, Habitual, Critical Readers* (2nd Ed.) Portsmouth, NH: Heinemann.

Barnhouse, D. & Vinton, V. (2012). *What Readers Really Do: Teaching the Process of Meaning Making.* Portsmouth, NH: Heinemann.

Beers, K. & Probst, R. (2012). *Notice & Note: Strategies for Close Reading.* Portsmouth, NH: Heinemann.

—. (2017). *Disrupting Thinking: Why How We Read Matters.* New York, NY: Scholastic.

Bennett, S. (2007). *That Workshop Book: New Systems and Structures for Classrooms That Read, Write, and Think.* Portsmouth, NH: Heinemann.

Booktrib. (n.d.) Retrieved from https://booktrib.com.

Cisneros, Sandra. (2015). *A House of My Own: Stories From My Life.* New York, NY: Knopf.

Coles, R. (1990). *The Call of Stories: Teaching and the Moral Imagination.* Boston, MA: Houghton Mifflin.

Crowder, T. & Nesloney, T. (2018). *Sparks in the Dark: Lessons, Ideas, and Strategies to Illuminate the Reading and Writing Lives in All of Us.* San Diego, CA: Dave Burgess Consulting, Inc.

Elbow, P. (1998). *Writing Without Teachers* (2nd Ed.). New York, NY: Oxford University Press.

Farrington, C.A., Roderick, M., Allensworth, E.,Nagaoka, J., Keyes, T.S. (2012). teaching adolescents to becomes learners: the role of noncognitive factors in shaping school performance. *The University of Chicago Consortium on Chicago School Research.*

Gallagher, K. (2004). *Deeper Reading: Comprehending Challenging Texts, 4–12.* Portland, ME: Stenhouse Publishers.

Gallagher, K. & Kittle, P. (2018). *180 Days: Two Teachers and the Quest to Engage and Empower Adolescents.* Portsmouth, NH: Heinemann.

Goldberg, G. & Houser, R. (2017). *What Do I Teach Readers Tomorrow? Fiction, Grades 3–8: Your Moment-to-Moment Decision-Making Guide.* Thousand Oaks, CA: Corwin.

Hartman, H.J. Instructional Science (1998). Vol. 26, No. 1/2, Special Issue: Metacognition in teaching and learning (MARCH 1998), pp. 1-3. Retreived from https://doi.org/10.1023/A:1003023628307.

Heard, G. (1998). *Awakening the Heart: Exploring Poetry in Elementary and Middle School.* Portsmouth, NH: Heinemann.

Jago, C. (2018). *The Book in Question: Why and How Reading Is in Crisis.* Portsmouth, NH: Heinemann.

Johnston, P. (2004). *Choice Words: How Our Language Affects Children's Learning.* Portland, ME: Stenhouse Publishers.

Keene, E. (2018). *Engaging Children: Igniting a Drive for Deeper Learning.* Portsmouth, NH: Heinemann.

Keene, E. & Zimmerman, S. (2007). *Mosaic of Thought: The Power of Comprehension Strategy Instruction* (2nd Ed.). Portsmouth, NH: Heinemann.

Kittle, P. (2012). *Book Love: Developing Depth, Stamina, and Passion in Adolescent Readers.* Portsmouth, NH: Heinemann.

LaGarde, J. & Crowder, T. (2018). Incombustible Ideas: The Subtle Bigotry of Book Banning. Retrieved from https://nerdybookclub.wordpress.com/2018/02/16/incombustible-ideas-the-subtle-bigotry-of-book-banning-by-jennifer-lagarde-and-travis-crowder/

Laminack, L. & Kelly, K. (2019). *Reading to Make a Difference: Using Literature to Help Students Speak Freely, Think Deeply, and Take Action.* Portsmouth, NH: Heinemann.

Latinxs in Kid Lit. (n.d.) Retrieved from https://latinosinkidlit.com.

Lehman, C. & Roberts, K. (2014). *Falling in Love with Close Reading: Lessons for Analyzing Texts—and Life.* Portsmouth, NH: Heinemann.

Lesesne, T. (2010). *Reading Ladders: Leading Students From Where They Are to Where We'd Like Them to Be.* Portsmouth, NH: Heinemann.

Maki, R. (2016). The Child Labor Coalition. ["ABCs of Child Labor" video]. Retrieved from stopchildlabor.org

Manguel, A. (2014). *A History of Reading.* New York, NY: Penguin Random House.

Miller, D. (2009). *The Book Whisperer: Awakening the Inner Reader in Every Child.* San Francisco, CA: Jossey-Bass.

Miller, D. & Kelly, S. (2013). *Reading in the Wild: The Book Whisperer's Keys to Cultivating Lifelong Reading Habits.* San Francisco, CA: Jossey-Bass.

Murray, D.M. (1981). making meaning clear: the logic of revision. *Journal of Basic Writing.* 03.3. 33-40.

Newkirk, T. (2011). *The Art of Slow Reading: Six Time-Honored Practices for Engagement.* Portsmouth, NH: Heinemann

—. (2014). *Minds Made for Stories: How We Really Read and Write Informational and Persuasive Texts.* Portsmouth, NH: Heinemann.

Pearson, P. D., Gallagher, M.C. (1983). The instruction of reading comprehension. *Comtemporary Educational Psychology*, 8, 317-344.

Probst, R.E. (1994). Reader-Response Theory and the English Curriculum. *The English Journal.* 83(3), 37-44. Retreived from http://www.csun.edu/~krowlands/Content/Academic_Resources/Literature/InstructionalStrategies/Probst-Readerresponse.pdf

—. (2004). *Response & Analysis: Teaching Literature in Secondary School* (2nd Ed.). Portsmouth, NH: Heinemann.

Pryle, M. (2018). *Reading with Presence: Crafting Meaningful, Evidence-Based Reading Responses*. Portsmouth, NH: Heinemann.

Rich in Color. (n.d.) Retrieved from http://richincolor.com.

Rief, L. (1991). *Seeking Diversity: Language Arts With Adolescents*. Portsmouth, NH: Heinemann.

—. (2007). *Inside the Writer's-Reader's Notebook: A Workshop Essential*. Portsmouth, NH: Heinemann.

—. (2014). *Read Write Teach: Choice and Challenge in the Reading-Writing Workshop*. Portsmouth, NH: Heinemann. Riffle Books. (n.d.) Retrieved from https://www.rifflebooks.com.

Rief. (2018) *The Quickwrite Handbook: 100 Mentor Texts to Jumpstart Your Students' Thinking and Writing*. Portsmouth, NH: Heinemann

Robb, L. (2000). *Teaching Reading in Middle School: A Strategic Approach to Teaching Reading That Improves Comprehension and Thinking*. New York, NY: Scholastic.

—. (2016). *Read Talk Write: 35 Lessons That Teach Students to Analyze Fiction and Nonfiction*. Thousand Oaks, CA: Corwin.

Roessing, L. (2009). *The Write to Read: Response Journals That Increase Comprehension*. Thousand Oaks, CA: Corwin.

Rosenblatt, L. (1995). *Literature as Exploration*. New York, NY: Modern Language Association.

Routman, R. (2018). *Literacy Essentials: Engagement, Excellence, and Equity for All Learners*. Portland, ME: Stenhouse Publishers.

School Library Journal. (n.d.) Retrieved from www.slj.com.

The Brown Bookshelf. (n.d.) Retrieved from https://thebrownbookshelf.com.

Thompson, M. (2001). *The Heart of the Mind*. Unionville, NY: Royal Fireworks Press.

Warner, J. (2018). *Why They Can't Write: Killing the Five-Paragraph Essay and Other Necessities*. Baltimore, MD: John Hopkins University Press.

Voice of Youth Advocates. (n.d.) Retrieved from voyamagazine.com.

We Need Diverse Books. (n.d.) Retrieved from diversebooks.org

Wilhelm, J. (2001). *Improving Comprehension With Think-Aloud Strategies: Modeling What Good Readers Do*. New York, NY: Scholastic.

Wolf, M. (2008). *Proust and the Squid: The Story and Science of the Reading Brain*. New York, NY: Harper Perennial.

Yates, K. & Nosek, C. (2018). *To Know and Nurture a Reader: Conferring With Confidence and Joy*. Portland, ME: Stenhouse Publishers.

Zuckerman, G. (2004). Development of Reflection Through Learning Activity. *European Journal of Psychology of Education*, 19, 9-18.

Children's Literature

Ahmed, S. (2019). *Internment*. New York, NY: Little, Brown and Co.

Alexander, K. (2015). *The Crossover*. New York, NY: Houghton Mifflin Harcourt Publishing Co.

Anderson, L.H. (2011). *Speak*. New York, NY: Square Fish/Macmillan.

—. (2019). *Shout*. New York, NY: Viking Books/Penguin Random House.

Bowling, D. (2017). *Insignificant Events in the Life of a Cactus*. New York, NY: Sterling Children's Books.

Boyne, J. (2007). *The Boy in the Striped Pajamas*. New York, NY: Penguin Random House.

Bradbury, R. (2013). *Fahrenheit 451*. New York, NY: Simon & Schuster.

Braden, Ann. (2018). *The Benefits of Being an Octopus*. New York, NY: Sky Pony Press/Skyhorse Publishing.

Brailler, M. & Holgate, D. (2015). *The Last Kids on Earth*. New York, NY: Penguin Random House.

Brown, D.J. (2014). *The Boys in the Boat: Nine Americans and Their Epic Quest for Gold at the 1936 Berlin Olympics*. New York, NY: Penguin Books.

Chaltas, T. (2010). *Because I Am Furniture*. New York, NY: Viking Books/Penguin Random House.

Cooney, C. (2010). *Three Black Swans*. New York, NY: Delacorte Press/Random House.

Creech, S. (2017). *Moo*. New York, NY: Harper Collins.

De la Peña, M. & Long, L. (2018). *Love*. New York, NY: G.P. Putnam's Sons/Penguin Random House.

Deuker, C. (2008). *Gym Candy*. New York, NY: Houghton Mifflin.

Dimaline, C. (2017). *The Marrow Thieves*. Toronto, Ontario: Cormorant Books, Inc.

Draper, S. (2012). Out of My Mind. New York, NY: Atheneum/Simon & Schuster.

Garber, Stephanie. (2017). *Caraval*. New York, NY: Flatiron Books/Macmillan Publishing,

Gino, A. (2017). *George*. New York, NY: Scholastic.

Gratz, A. (2017). *Refugee*. New York, NY: Scholastic.

Hahn, M.D. (2017). *Took*. New York, NY: Clarion Books/Houghton Mifflin Harcourt.

Hinton, S.E. (2006). *The Outsiders*. New York, NY: Speak/Penguin Random House.

House, S. (2002). *Clay's Quilt*. Ballantine Books/Penguin Random House.

Howard, G. (2019). *The Whispers*. New York, NY: G.P. Putnam's Sons/Penguin Random House.

Kiely, E. (2018). *Tradition*. New York, NY: Margaret K. McElderry Books/Simon & Schuster.

Kingsolver, B. (1999). *The Poisonwood Bible*. New York, NY: Harper Perennial.

Kinney, J. (2007). *Diary of a Wimpy Kid*. New York, NY: Amulet Books/Abrams.

Lee, H. (2005). *To Kill a Mockingbird*. New York, NY: Harper Perennial.

Lê, M. & Santat, D. (2018). *Drawn Together*. New York, NY: Hyperion/Disney Group.

Lowry, L. (1993). *The Giver*. New York, NY: Houghton Mifflin Harcourt.

McCain, G. & McNeil, L. (2016). *Dear Nobody: The True Diary of Mary Rose*. Naperville, IL: Sourcebooks.

McCullough, J. (2018). *Blood Water Paint*. New York, NY: Dutton Books/Penguin Random House.

Melleby, Nicole. (2019). *Hurricane Season*. Chapel Hill, NC: Algonquin Young Readers/ Workman Publishing Co.

Montgomery, S. (2016). *The Soul of an Octopus: A Surprising Exploration Into the Wonder of Consciousness*. New York, NY: Atria/Simon & Schuster.

Morrison, T. (2004). *Beloved*. New York, NY: Vintage Books/Random House.

Noah, T. (2017). *Born a Crime: Stories from a South African Childhood*. New York, NY: Random House.

O'Sullivan, J. (2017). *Between Two Skies*. Somerville, MA: Candlewick Press.

Palacio, R.J. (2012). *Wonder*. New York, NY: Alfred A. Knopf/Random House.

Pan, E.X.R. (2018) *The Astonishing Color of After*. Boston, MA: Little, Brown & Co.

Park, L. (2011). *A Long Walk to Water: Based on a True Story*. New York, NY: Clarion Books/ Houghton Mifflin Harcourt.

Probst, R. (2004) *Response and Analysis,* 2E. Portsmouth, NH: Heinemann

Saeed, A. (2018). *Amal Unbound*. New York, NY: Nancy Paulsen Books/Penguin Random House.

Sarles, S. & Patterson, J. (2018). Campfire. New York, NY: James Patterson Books/Little, Brown and Co.

Schmidt, G. (2017). *Orbiting Jupiter*. New York, NY: Clarion Books/Houghton Mifflin Harcourt.

Sepetys, R. (2012). *Between Shades of Gray*. New York, NY: Penguin Books.

Slater, D. (2017). *The 57 Bus: The True Story of Two Teenagers and the Crime That Changed Their Lives*. New York, NY: Macmillan.

Smith, A. (2014). *Winger*. New York, NY: Simon & Schuster.

—. (2016). *Stand-Off*. New York, NY: Simon & Schuster.

Stevenson, B. (2015). *Just Mercy: A Story of Justice and Redemption*. New York, NY: Penguin Random House.

Stone, N. (2018). *Dear Martin*. New York, NY: Ember/Random House.

Telegemeier, R. (2010). *Smile*. New York, NY. Scholastic.

Thomas, A. (2017). *The Hate U Give*. New York, NY: Harper Collins.

Warner, J. (2018). *Why They Can't Write: Killing the Five-Paragraph Essay and Other Necessities*. Baltimore, MD: John Hopkins University Press.

Woodson, J. (2016). *Brown Girl Dreaming*. New York, NY: Puffin Books/Penguin Random House.

X.R. Pan, E. (2018). *The Astonishing Color of After*. New York, NY: Little, Brown and Co.

Zafon, C. R. (1964). *The Shadow of the Wind*. New, York, NY: Penguin Books.

Zoboi, I. (2017). *American Street*. New York, NY: Harper Collins.

Zusak, M. (2007). *The Book Thief*. New York, NY: Alfred A. Knopf/Random House.

